EXACTING CLAM No. 6 — Autumn 2022

I0667972

CONTENTS

Front cover: "I Didn't Carry a Watermelon" by John Patrick Higgins

© 2022 Sagging Meniscus Press
All Rights Reserved
ISBN: 978-1-952386-49-7

Exacting Clam is a quarterly publication from Sagging Meniscus.

Senior Editors: Aaron Anstett, Jesi Bender, Jeff Chon, Elizabeth Cooperman, Tyler C. Gore, Charles Holdefer, Kurt Luchs, M.J. Nicholls, Doug Nufer, Thomas Walton

Executive Editor: Guillermo Stitch

Publisher: Jacob Smullyan

exactingclam.com

Benjamin McPherson Ficklin

Your momentary/ eternal name

He's dreaming of her and jazz: somebody's playing trumpet in a shadowy stadium, she's lost somewhere in the rows of seats, maybe not concealed, maybe simply listening to the somber melody, the sorrowful timbre of the trumpeter's music, air in lungs, the shape of their mouth, the rising and pressing of their fingers, this ancient stadium of stone that's filled with a sadness that he, our dreamer, cannot bear, vanquished, he sits, tries to focus on the music, realizes she's somewhere nearby yet forever lost because that's where she wants to exist, or perhaps she's sitting with the woman from the previous night, the woman from London visiting Japan with her cousin, the woman who loves being a surgeon even though she said it was taxing, the Black woman in the silver dress with long braids who kissed her as it switched from year to year, then the dreams shifts and he's a starship, he's aboard a starship but sees it from space, he's deserted the armada, he's fleeing through the cosmos while the trumpeter continues, he's run from enslavement as castle-brick-brusher or labyrinth-wall-smoother or grain-of-sand-picker-upper, he's left his numerical designation #676 to search for a name in the event horizon of the closening black hole, he's been dishonored, de-personified by the galactic kingdom, which is acceptable as long as there's an instant before being shredded into elementary particles when he realizes his name again, not a sound or a symbol, but his name of names of ever changing names that used to feel so near, he's in its gravitational pull now, and he realizes that he's forgotten his

family, that the shame and suffering he's left his parents with is a selfishness, and he wonders if it's better to live in shame or die, a toilet flushes, his eyes open, he looks to his bed/couch and sees that she's missing, he sits up from the mat on the floor, he's still wearing his suit, his head hurts, he feels so embarrassed/alone, and in the bathroom with her head bowed in the toilet bowl, she hears the bell outside keep ringing, she feels selfish to the point of self-loathing, and in this moment of waiting to see if she'll puke again, her thoughts are concrete: I abandoned my revolution over a woman that didn't love me back, I fled the battle to treat an imagined wound in a country far away from the targeted drone strikes and murderous fascists, I am hungover in a strange apartment, I am an abject piece of shit, she pukes again, finds the flush button on the toilet's arm, slides open the door, reenters the studio apartment's main room, a bell rings outside, Good morning, he says, still sitting on his floor mat in his suit with red eyes and disheveled hair, Morning, she says, self-conscious that she's wearing jeans and a bra, You put on Chet Baker, he says, the first side of the records is over, the vinyl rotates soundlessly, Oh yeah, I didn't want you to hear me puke, he doesn't know what to say, she walks to the tiny kitchen area and pours herself a glass of water, Good idea, he turns from her toward his window and the huge snowy mountain rising out of the urban infinity, she sits back on the couch, I'm sorry you don't feel good, Thanks, I don't feel good either, and the bell rings outside again, they sit there, she on his bed/couch with her eyes closed and the glass cup of water in her pale hands, he propped up on his floor mat with his eyes on the mountain, outside the bell continues to ring in regular pairs: two quick gongs before silencing, letting the traffic noise take over again, he remembers holding the hands of his parents on another New Years Day, he remembers standing in line at the white shrine with all the red flags and the fruit-bearing citrus trees, the wooden prayer cards rattling in the wind, he remembers approaching with his parents on either side of him, clapping twice, bowing, gripping the thick rope and ringing the bell twice, tossing the yen coins into the grate, meanwhile she's debating love vs. revolution, owing one's self vs. owing humanity, fighting for your life vs. the lives of others, self-perseverance vs. self-sacrifice, dying in battle to the last person vs. survival in isolated exile, love in the days of death vs. celibacy in the fight for life, he imagines them the same pole of different magnets, she worries that he wants her to leave, so she says, Thank you so much for letting me crash here, You're welcome, it's nice to have company on New Year, Even if that company makes you sleep on the floor of your apartment? and he chuckles and says I don't mind, That's kind of you, Why didn't you go home with the British lady from the club? she takes another sip of water and says, Honestly because she probably wanted to hook up and I'm not trying to fuck anybody right now, he laughs again and feels his fingers begin to dissolve, Did you see Mount Fuji? What? he points and says, Mount Fuji, and she leans toward him and he smells cigarettes and humanity, she smells cologne and humanity, That's beautiful, and she feels stronger amidst insignificance, Want some water, she asks, Yes please, and she gets them each a glass of water and flips the record, What's that bell that keeps ringing? A shrine, What do you mean? Families go to the shrines for New Years Day, and sitting back down on the bed/couch, she asks, Why aren't you? and pain contorts his face, sorrow, he turns toward the mountain, Today is my first New Year with no family, and he remembers standing over the calm face of his dead father and realizing, only after taking the train across Japan, that there was nothing he could do to bring his father back, she pets down his sleeve, finds his fingers, holds them, I'm sorry, It's okay, Well it doesn't have to be okay, he turns toward her, My grandpa died two years ago and it still doesn't feel okay, or I guess I mean it's okay that it hurts, it'll always hurt, and he turns toward her with tears in his eyes, Thank you for saying that, she squeezes his hand and he squeezes back, he, for some reason, thinks of how there is no such thing as the center of the Universe, the bell keeps ringing, stopping, ringing again, a deep full sound, Chet Baker keeps playing trumpet, Are you in Japan to party for New Year? and she chuckles, No, a woman in LA broke my heart, and my fucking country is falling apart, and I haven't been able to get any of my art done, I guess I don't know really, I'm trying to figure out what's wrong, and he says, I think I understand, and she, for some reason, thinks of people crossing the Pacific in massive canoes, What art do you do? Graffiti mostly, Do you remember last night coming here on the train and telling me to quit my job, and she laughs hard and says, No, and he laughs, too, and says, This morning I am thinking about it, and she descends from the bed/couch and wraps her arms between his cotton shirt and jacket, tucks her legs into his, buries her face into his shoulder, and says, Can we lie just like this until we feel a little bit better? Yes, he says, Then can we go to the shrine? Yes, he smiles, watching a few clouds pass over infinity, Is that okay? Of course it is okay, why not? I mean maybe because I don't know what any of it means, To me, he says, closing his eyes, I mostly think of it as praying for a good New Year, Cool, she says, closing her eyes, the world could use a good New Year, Plus you will be with me, Plus I'll be with you, and they lie there listening to the bell and the jazz, they lie there for another hour in each other's forevers, they lie there nearing their momentary names.

P.J. Blumenthal

Program Music from a Coming War

(Chorus for eleven voices)

What war?
—Jean Marais

I

This is my farewell to history.

Half my life is already past and still I haven't said what I mean.

The time is growing short.

Already the drought has struck Europe, and soon the crops will die from heat and lack of water, all that is except the grapes which thrive on the sun and the deeper moisture, and there shall be only grapes to eat and wine to drink.

From this a moral issue will arise, and from this moral issue, a new war, a war different from any before; a war that has previously existed only in art and for which there has never been a precedent in time. Intoxication shall battle the sixty centuries that have banded together under the name of history. The banks of the Rhine and the Mosel shall flood with a mingling of blood and wine.

No one can say yet which side they'll be on. The battle lines will be full of surprises. The war will have no respect for nationalities or political loyalties. These will crack apart like the dry earth in which the wheat lies withering.

No appeal to sentiment will have any meaning. Lives shall not be the barter of this war. The phonies will not beseech the phony hearts. They won't even try. The economy of this war shall not be measured in the dead but in the living.

The fighting shall spread quickly to the Americas and Asia and all the islands between. Nothing shall escape the ferocity.

I cannot stay silent any longer. It is impossible to hold back the flow.

I have hesitated too long, and I do not want the slaughter on my conscience. Perhaps it is too late.

The war will show no mercy. Liabilities will have no names but their own. It is ridiculous to challenge this.

Whoever denies the urgency will shriek to hear the chorus of exiles which magnified through a thousand megaphones is barely audible except through concentrated listening.

Run to the monitors and see the prisoners of light.

The issue is not credibility. The issue is not politics: nor is it economics. Only procrastinators and profiteers will call these structures grammatical.

The issue is war and nothing else. Explain it as you may. It will not change the body count.

I must tell you it's coming. I must tell you everything I know. You may believe me or not.

Already the drought hangs over Europe. The sun weighs down. Heat has lost its friendliness. Friends and strangers are rumoring. The threat of leadership is upon us.

How to emphasize the urgency? How to convince you I am serious? Whoever hesitates is his own executioner, and maybe yours.

II

No one remembers why the war is being fought. Even the names of the generals are a matter of dispute and the cause of much spilled blood.

Couriers run loudly down long corridors. One hears only footsteps in the wake of their haste.

Reports from the front are geometric: acute angles, ellipses, square-talk, a voice in an unknown language speaking in parables.

Who stained the tiles! someone cries.

The clock! The clock!

A functionary points and other functionaries stare.

Clack Clack Clack Clack Clack.

Everything disappears behind a door except for a sharp line of shadow.

The radio switches on.

Particles of light and darkness are all that remain of sound disintegration.

A hand reaches out and grabs yours squeezing to the feather lines of your most delicate calibrations.

You look up and out. The whites of your eyes are whiter than I've ever seen them before.

You are afraid. You don't recognize me at first. Music is all you care for and electricity. You try to flee but I do not let go. I pull you away. Outdoors. You resist. You try not to touch me. You know what this meeting means. You squirm in my hands. You do not want to say who I am.

You say:

Let us keep one mystery at least.

Anything else, I smile, but not this one.

III

A Happy End

I was sixteen when we met. You stood there cocky and smirking as if I should know who you were. You told me you worked for the railroad, that you had nothing to do with the sea.

Your breath smelled of crocuses. I fed you flowers. I had never seen a white bull before. You let me stroke your forehead. Your horns were small and pale and smooth like ivory. You held out your breast to be caressed. I had never felt such soft hair, so fine, finer than cat fur. You lumbered through the meadow and I along with you. You nodded your head and knelt beside me. I dared to climb on your back.

Before I knew, you had carried me off to your ship. You tore off my girlish smock and touched my breasts. I tingled with fear. And then you threw me rudely on the bed. At first the pain was sharp but then I wouldn't let you go, wrapping my legs around your back to keep you there.

Suddenly I was thirty and my children were growing up. We lived in sixpence beds from Ceylon to the South China Sea. You came home drunk if you came home at all, and then with the smell of perfume on your neck. You called me by the names of other women when you handled me in bed. And yet I washed your shirts and paid your gambling debts when the boatswains knocked on the door, and I cut your hair when it grew too long and polished your shoes and taught the children to read.

And then one day you left. You were going to the tobacco shop you said. You kissed me goodbye. You smelled of whiskey and your beard scratched my cheek. You walked out the door slapped our son in the face and told him he'd better not be a wiseguy.

I won't say how many years went by, and I don't think it matters. Nor how many times I stood at the harbor thinking your ship might pull in while the harbor rats grabbed at me and called me names not even you ever dared to. My hair turned white as the cresting waves and my bones began to crack in the salty wind. But all I heard was the roar of the cranes and the crashing of goods into the hatch and voices of thousands of bums like you asking young girls for a light.

Even now I sit by the shore, like a pillar of salt. The ships sail past my eyes and then away. I imagine the breeze is carrying a message I cannot understand. I know that is a lie. Still I would like to believe it. Perhaps you will return. And perhaps I will not take you back. Who can say? And what are the memories worth anyway? The children are gone. They will not wait as I have. They will not love you as I have. They think I am a silly old woman. They talk about expediency. Let them laugh. Let them say what they want. I am used to waiting. Who can judge the depth of these things? Who really knows what this means and what certainties will be revealed through foolish perseverance?

IV

Oh hell. Then loose the demons with the angels.

I am beautiful. There is no doubt.

I cannot double my meanings anymore.

Night has fallen on the city that is the symbol of the soul, and thousands of indwelling opinions, embodied, classed and fit with histories fill the bars, movie houses, bordellos and restaurants with delicate obscenities.

Give the whiners a break too for once and the loud ones and the dreamers with deadly surprises in store.

For heaven's sake see how they stream from occupation to preoccupation: the smallest movement unavoidably consequent: relatives scattered in all corners of the globe. Post a daily matter.

O beloved, look into my light. It is night now. I am beautiful.

See, what looks like silken skin is writhing with life.

Those are not ornaments, are not removable—not one.

Steal a single piece and you have killed the whole.

V

Alba

I recall the details better than my name, what perfume you were wearing, how your dress was fringed at the wrist, even your earrings: simple pearl teardrops, and how you said, "like our love," and how we laughed. It was not until later that I learned what a sacrifice it had been and that you were suffering from a colic and had hidden the pain. My uncle had a high position in the government and was very much in favor of the war; you were from a long line of social democrats. I always wondered how we'd met.

We spent the night on the hillside, looking down into the city, its shadows, flickering lights and bells: and the sky was dark and the stars so plentiful we manufactured new constellations and called them by each other's names and said that they should have their rightful place with the others, as permanent as the Zodiac or Orion or the Pleiades.

And your tongue was sweet when we kissed and your breath cool as the wind that hunted through the grass. And many times we swore it could never end, and we prayed we might grow together like trees or die in each other's arms. We must have laughed half the night out of sheer disbelief that it was really happening. And once you even said, "What more is there than this?" And I had no answer until the dawn.

VI

At first it was a low murmuring, and no one took it seriously. A few crackpots they said. There are always a few.

The shops were filled with goods and the change in weather, although irregular, was hailed by some as a boon, the herald of a new age. Some called it the return to the garden and predicted that before long orange groves would stretch far beyond Lübeck, and avocados would grow in every yard. Clubs formed to reverence the sun, and many joined them shedding their clothes and browning their skins religiously. Even the farmers hailed the changes, claiming with sun like that and a little more rain, it could be the best harvest in years.

But the rains didn't come, and the murmuring grew, and soon the crackpots were proliferating until you couldn't tell who the crackpots were and who the patriots.

When the rivers dried up and the cattle slaughtered for lack of feed and sold dirt cheap on the market for the little they'd bring in, and the wheat and the rye wilted on the stalk, and the corn was dwarfed, the cry for a victim became audible. Even to the councilors. A victim? Why a victim? Nothing could be more absurd. But though the councilors knew that, they also knew someone had to take the blame. But who? It was a question of them or us and then only a question of finding them.

VII

Everyone knew a hero was on the way, but nobody knew his name or where he might come from or what he would exact as a price for her salvation. Would he trample on the hollow monuments, those reminders that the need to build is native to every age? Would he speak of the hallowed past and imagine it in printed words? Or would he be an agent of the speculators and barter real estate for temporary gain? No direction he might come from was free of interpretation. Danger from the east. Suspicion from the west. Death from the north and surrender from the south.

VIII

The Dead Poets

They manufacture truth in our names, turn our fallibilities into guidelines and curse coming generations with our tedious histories.

Who can enjoy the spirit of the thing without the academic burden?

What if we communicated on another frequency?

Europe can you read us? We are the voices that remain of your past. A choir of renown, architects of libraries and significance, as nameless as cathedral builders, our signatures pressed into the mortar of cultural history. From Poitiers to London from Bonn to Florence and Prague. Each time you call our names we serve you, doomed to be dragged down into the fields of gravity.

Speak of us with care.

We were generous when we were among you.

Be generous to us now.

We took a chance. We profaned the spirit of the age. We carried on a war of love and hate against form and principle.

We ask only the same in return.

IX

I did not think the war would go this far. I did not know it was so serious. The knife and the wound are irretractable. The insults have already cut deep.

I was born to lead a burgher's life, I thought, not fit for war, confused by adversity, measuring days with superstitious regularity and calculating action by arithmetic.

Until the coming of the railroad our village had no contact with the sea. We celebrate those times in festivals now that have grown to depend on electricity and in street names and family names and fables that have lost their controversy.

For years I dreamed of disasters, shuddered at the imaginings. My thoughts filled with mishaps splashed on the sidewalk like the blood of accident victims.

But that was fantasy, erasable, gnostic dabblings, visionary states.

Why is there nowhere to vacation now away from this field of conflict, no summer comfort, no lover whose hand you hold in a reckless state of truce, not even a pleasant superstition anymore, tight as a priest's collar and as certain as preterition?

Will no one offer me the safety my little war denies? Will you wait to read about my death in papers or see my body on a screen wrapped in plastic while images of the dead and body counts fade in and out of focus? And when it is over, will you speak about us to your friends, or maybe send a donation or write a book that will assure you a career or meditate at the places we fell to still a hunger for pilgrimages?

Will no one not be fooled by all this heartache? Or will you accept my fate without argument as easily as your own?

X

A Suicide Note

The only light is from the moon. It crosses the bed obliquely.

They sleep without touching and call it a by name that has been written in older books.

A column of cigarette smoke rises towards the window. Music on the radio.

Why can't we breed anymore in Europe? Shall all our children be Turks and Hindoos? The moon is in a barren sign and everyone's talking about God.

I was born to be a hero but of that promise only the prophecy is left and the unbreachable separation between actor and act.

God what I wouldn't give for the sea today, to be balanced at its very edge precariously and permanently: that thin endless strip that is neither wet nor dry but shares the quality of both.

But I am landlocked: a longing face framed by windowpanes.

It was my wish to leave a testament, but I shall not. It was my wish to leave a warning, but that too I won't. It was my wish to write long sentences, but only the words are long and instead of the sea, I am balanced on a knife.

Let's get on with it. Enough of this chatter, this last attempt to frame the problem in images.

The last picture is a target, the only visibility left.

I shall not wait for the mail today.

Strike!

Blood and truth shall mix at least once.

XI

Without warning the day exploded into symbols.

There was no resisting the force of that displacement.

Some made the effort, but it was in vain, and all the people of Europe were transformed from people you meet on the street and in the shops and offices to the people you meet in dreams.

Nobody's name was just a name but the echo of words that had other meanings, and Tom and Gisela and Marie were emanations of the truth, tense presences, messengers, wandering the shifting scenery of significance. No place was spared meaning nor any sentence. Every word was a cover for other words. Alternate meanings dwelled in the shadow of every utterance in the languages of Europe.

Some blamed it on Television, others on the Computer or the Petroleum Industry and the accessibility of the outer provinces. Others claimed it was the angels or the devils.

But who could really explain this dehydration?

A malaria of the atmosphere? A dysentery of the soul?

The councilors of Europe gathered at her sickbed. They came from every edge and centrality of the dry continent. They gave her water to drink, rubbed glycerin on her lips and oils on her body and talked among each other in whispers. I'm afraid we've gone too far this time, they said. If she goes now, it'll mean the end of us.

Two Poems

Negative Confession

I am not:

lazy susan with 3 wood-marbled ceramic trays of extra- high gloss waiting to be turned
to you: blousy, fermented spritzer under maidenform for your intoxication, relief

tree chalice sans french sibilants woody undertones, absent of flowers
raw innocence under it all waiting for cream to calm

ocular salt welling, expectorant to liquid dust with the dam break you've coquetted
cracked interiority bathed in melanated oil dermi

buying into a fire deity to acidate my infinite coil killing the hierophant water spiritessa
as from bowels below fungi and demise as I have obviously always surfaced

desiring anything on my cranial perception cornered as my senses are full, never
less perceived as underfed except where men choose to eat, suckle, succumb.

Nighttime is the ___ time

as it collapses like it does for retirees their third year off
so do hours. Last time I was home and thinking, besides
this time, all the time, I saw things in my house. Things I'd bought:
A series of plants that make a sculptured imprint in air, my still
African art, a cheap trinket I bought for this year's Lunar New Year.

The Rat year is supposed to be new. It is. Sometimes I see my cat's
eyes scurry to a corner and I wonder what's there. The precision
of their look. Once I got on the ground behind one so close the
twitched ears began to lie, I wondered what spectrum of sight he
had that saw what thing move. He don't blink but as the whiskers
fritter with his breath there's a silence of knowing that trains him
to eat or play with something to death.

I notice unattributable breezes at home. Windows closed, ivy
shivers along the top, even the heavy-edged snake one that
defies gravity. the bamboo one, asparagus struggling to fern.
The sticks in them a reminder of dry days, almost straw among
the small pin prick leaves. A poinsettia with holiday paper still around it.
A festive time. Besides those small wind tunnels everything is immobile.
Except for the whiskers everything is stilted. Except for what I can't see,
nothing pulses.

DAVID ROSE

MING

She is happy; we are happy.

It has lasted a good while now. I do want it to continue.

I should finish dressing. I am pink from the shower, in just a shirt, slumped in a wicker chair. I feel, probably look, like a figure in a Bacon painting.

The velvet jacket and the elastic bow tie are on the bed. Ginette chose them. She buys all my clothes. She has laid them out before going on to the dinner, early.

The jacket, certainly, is laid out, its arms crossed. I think of Satie's dozen identical velvet suits. Satie . . . sartorial... sardonic...

Ginette hates wordplay, anything that smacks of irony. I tried to explain to her its emollient properties. Ironic— irenic. There you go again, she shouted.

In parts of China, babies are tied into sacks of mud while t mothers work in the fields. I read about it this morning. Th ractice has been criticized. Child experts talk of stunted gro h, physically and emotionally. I must say it struck me too as r embling the cultivation of Bonsai. I had a vision of paddy fiel dotted with little sacked saplings, waving in the wind.

Bu he mothers maintain that it's perfectly healthy. The moist si t is softer than any nappy, comforting, probably sensual. An ey get used to it.

I shan't, w, be able to work a wet clay, mix a slip, without thinking planted cherubs.

It is normal Ginette's thighs I am reminded of. Or the other way round— r thighs remind me of wet clay; I catch myself reworking the y's pot in the après-sex.

On bad days it i y first pot I think of. Not working it but dropping it.

Days like today.

You never forget your rst pot. Not your first attempt, but your first real pot, th ne that happens when something within you conspires with th lay to catch you unawares, presenting you with a form that's ect; something both yours and not yours, like a child.

There are other pots, better ts, but they're not your first.

My first I can still feel in m ands. It was a simple Chinese form, although I didn't know th at the time. It was made at school, under the nodding bird-li tention of Mr. Ray. He helped me glaze it, handed me the ton like a nurse to a surgeon; fussed over the firing. He seemed as roud as I was.

It was entered for Prize Day and the Gover r's Award.

I don't recall what triggered it. Somethi trivial, no doubt. I just remember the pot bellied in my han the glaze cold and creamy to my fingers as I let it sli through. Feeling in my viscera the slow-motion smash.

I have twenty minutes to dress and get a tax Ginette impressed on me the need to be punctual. It wasn't eas or her, she had to do it without letting out that I'm the Gue of Honour. Actually I've known for weeks. She's out of her th with deception. She was quite flustered trying to exp n the dinner jacket. And why she had to get there ahead of me

There's time for a drink though. A small one. A gine She hates that joke. She suspects it of irony. I tell r it's just a pun.

Irony is different; serious. It's a way of parting mpany with fate, of running, for a while, on a parallel t ck, of disengaging.

But women, I find, have no sense of irony. Helen h n't, nor had Susan.

I told Helen I was happy being miserable; she ok it as ironic.

I told Susan she would be better off with som ne else; she thought I was being noble, or self-pitying, or

Tell a woman you love her and she suspects rcasm at the least.

As it turns out, Susan is better off wi someone else. There was a fellow student of hers—a fello f hers, a student of mine—I thought would be good for her. s pots were usually dumpy earthenware things, like a ploughma hands (like his own hands, in fact). That's always a good s n. If it's reliability you're looking for.

 EXACTING CLAM

But she found someone else e   rely. Eventually. I was genuinely pleased for her, despite   e pain. And soon after came the small British Council displ   of my work in Germany. I had been afraid of turning it down   ut it went ahead.

Fifteen minutes.

That was how I came to   et Helen. She did the translation of the catalogue. She   se to come to my studio each time she was stuck on a technical   erm, lugging a dictionary in a raffia bag, like a baby in a c   rycot.

Then she just k   coming.

She told me her   vourite artist was Klee. I said that was a good omen. It wa   she was good for me.

She had a p   icular interest in Bauhaus design. We went back to Germany   few months after the exhibition, to Dessau and Dornburg,   study their pottery.

Under   s influence, I moved away from delicate, lathe-turned   to something more sculptural. That's when I produced my 'Kl   -vase'—tall, fluted, decorated with his leaf and moon moti   It turned out to be one of my most successful works, but in   ct, the vase acquired by the Ceramic Guild was a slightly ea   er version. The first one was broken.

We had had an argument, or rather we hadn't; I accused Helen o   suspecting me of an affair. I knew she didn't, and she knew I k   w.

She   elped me pick up the pieces, and by then it had passed. e made   love and planned another trip.

We   w   e planning a trip a few months later, ironically enough (da   I say it?). The gourd-like shapes I was producing in respons   to the Bauhaus influence had led me to a deeper study of Ara   c ceramics. I said I'd like to go to Syria. She wanted to go   Tunisia—where Klee had first experienced colour, as she pu   t. We agreed to compromise and go to Egypt.

In the event,   wrote and said why didn't we each go where we really wanted to   separately, and remain like that?

I remember tearin   he sheet of paper from my sketchpad for the letter.

Why, I wonder, is i   called cartridge paper? Is there a connection with bullets?   eems appropriate. I always use cartridge paper for Dear Jan

Ten minutes. I could sti   make it.

I gather I'm to receive the   ard Leach Memorial Award and Travel Grant. I am, of course, *not   posed to know.*

I could use it to go to Syria. I   ver did get there.

A toast of my own. Ginette! I   n it, really. There's nothing I wouldn't do for her.

I've never been one for diaries.   e temptation of the confessional is one I usually find easy   resist. I keep a notebook though. A series of bound sketchpads,   vering most of my working life. I record my best pieces—   lour-washed drawings, details of glazes, firing temperatures, s   s. And a page at the back for breakages.

I was going through them last night. I made an in   esting discovery: the earlier stages of my relationships—as fa   s I am able to date them—correlate with an output of porcela   , paper-thin, with brushed transparent glazes.

Maybe that says something about the fragility of happiness Or its dryness.

At any rate, it usually gives way, after six months o   m   e, to stone or earthenware, in primitive or biomorphic   apes with dipped glazes, or decoration in slip, *sgraffito*   r wax resist. Followed by a clutch of increasingly heavy   extures   netted, pebbled, corrugated, gouged.

Then a return to finer work, and an equilibriu   etween the two.

I tried a cross-reference with the breakage   but they are not all dated, and besides, they weren't broken i   sequence.

I still have seven minutes, and my trouse   s.

My socks are laid out on the bed like foren   c exhibits, in case I wear a mismatched pair. They are black   lk, with a silver motif, a sort of Aztec design. Ginette's id   of craft-chic.

To be fair, though, her choice was proba   prompted by my current work. I have become fascinated wit   arly Peruvian ware. I am turning out stoneware bowls a   plates with incised geometric designs or stylised relief-m   lling. I spent all last month experimenting with salt-gla   techniques. There's a particular texture I am after—   rser than orange-peel, and highly lustred.

I have tried combinations   slips, overlaid in trails or double-dipped; increased the   ron oxide; used rapid-cooling techniques. It's beginning bear fruit, but so far, there's nothing exceptional, nothi that warms the solar plexus.

So the problem, aga is, I've nothing in reserve.

I had the problem year ago. I had produced a series of enamelled porcelain b s, lidded, like Fabergé eggs. But I had already sold the f st three, and the rest, though adequate, lacked something. T y had, to me, the feel of copies, they could have been in strial ware. I was beginning to crave a return to the sl and coiled work I had been doing the year before; before inette.

As luck uld have it, I was offered a teaching post at the Northern, s ething I had been angling for. It came at the right time. I t ned it down.

I ld Ginette it was for our sake, so as not to be parted. I r ise now that was true.

I feel very warm. I suppose from the shower. Perhaps I should leave her a note and go for a walk.

he paper feels oddly, subtly, wrong under my fingerpads. It grained, rough. It feels expectant, like biscuitware awaitin glaze.

It shou feel smooth, creamy. It should feel like the first pot.

On second t ughts, the pot should feel like the paper.

As a child, best ever birthday present was a sketchpad of thick cartridge per I had been used to practising my drawing on cardboard, c eal packets, anything I could get hold of.

I took the sketchpad n a field trip to the churchyard, and worked all afternoon. It ook several attempts, but the final drawing—sunwashed steepl carefully stippled foliage—pleased me, elated me.

At home, I peeled it from e pad, intending to frame it with glass and passepartout.

A day or so later, I was told f. I was late for tea, I remember. I went up to my room; I pi ed up the drawing, still unmounted, and tore it in two, very owly. The tear thrilled across the paper. I put the pieces gether, and tore them again, the other way. A ritual disembowe ng.

Two minutes to zero-hour.

Ginette will be round straight after the , possibly before. She will conduct a post-mortem on the ja t. She will comment on the glazed look on my face, and I will b le to say, triumphantly, now who's being ironic?

Tonic? I think so, this time.

My watch beeps from the bathroom. The decision is ure now.

I feel myself settling in, nestling down into e silt, silky between my toes, my legs, around my waist, I wave acr s the Yangtze.

This time, though, I feel virtu s.

This is for you, sweethea .

M.J. NICHOLLS

THE State of Texas: A Travelogue

I arrived at Houston airport following a stuporous flight from London at nine in the am, UTC. The travelling experience, the usual anting hither and heck to secure spinal caries on benches and thrombosis in long-moaning lines of wait, was ameliorated by the first-class treatment afforded me by my publisher, Strident Arena, who were banking on the success of this travelogue to lift them into debt. I had taken an experimental sooper-soother (sic) medicament recommended me by Dr. Bill Waxter (no relation to my poet friend Mr. Will Baxter, whose raucous verse has never nestled within the warm clam of two paperboards), a practitioner from Austin who co-concocted a new form of chill pill—a sedative retro-sprinkled with lisdexamfetamine to create a tantalising mellow with surprising palatal pips. I was on a two-week trial, having read with interest the doctor's astute piece on the use of remdesivir in halting athlete's foot while bathing in untreated water. This state was perfect for taxiing past the demerara knolls and prominent pylons of Westfield, the cool waft of a spring Texas breeze pleasing the parallel strips of red oak and redbuds, as I hurtled towards the Mountain Goats Motel in Pasadena for a nine-hour recline.

In addition to rescuing the perilous finances of my publisher, I had come to Texas to immerse myself in "the basket case of America" (as opposed to the Midwest, i.e. the breadbasketcase of America) to understand how the average American citizen managed to drag themselves out of bed when around 45% of the population walk around packing heat with no access to mental health professionals and politicians who tell folks to lock and load their cares away. I had no intention to write a winsome frolic on the strange manners of these kook-laced New Worlders, to compose homilies to hominy, paeans to popsicles, or big-ups to barbecue ribs, nor was I interested in rocking up to Trump rallies raising a quizzical brow to the riotous thickness of the masses, or spending Therouvian weird weekends with quirk merchants with tragic futures. I had arranged to speak to several so-called disrupters, the leaders of various resistance movements bubbling under the surface in Texas. Awaking in my protocynical motel—the American equivalent of a Travelodge, with 40% more murk—I speedily showered and powered to meet Kay Alabaster, the extraordinary woman whose efforts in foetal smuggling I would experience firsthand in the following text-blocks.

I met Kay, a fiercer incarnation of Holly Hunter in stature and visage, in a verge ten versts from the headquarters of The Society of Liberated Almost-Persons (SLAP), a terrifying dystopian compound located strategically on the Texas-Louisiana border. Disguised as an Amazon "fulfilment" centre—an artless rectangular slab of commerce minus the fusillade of lorries pouring from becalmed loading bays—the compound had been actioned by Texan senator Broomley Hawkwhip, a furious protector of the unborn. Inside was an army-style makeshift hospital, where pregnant women caught trying to leave the state for abortions were held hostage by ex-military Christian wingnuts with guns trained on their temples as they passed the time watching TV on a series of shonky beds. Ever since abortion was made illegal in Texas, neighbouring states had set up "abortion Ubers", expensive hire cars taking women to clinics for their procedures and returning them home. Many of the drivers were nurses earning extra crust after shifts, popular for the aftercare they were able to provide to the stressed or traumatised patients. Identifying the common routes to the out-of-state clinics, Hawk-whip had deployed border patrol to catch the offending Ubers, arrest the drivers, and reroute (kidnap) the women to their "holding centre", where they were held until the babies were born. Once they'd had their children, the women were removed from the site and prodded onto the roads with their babies swaddled in a complimentary shawl, where they had to walk home, hitch a ride, or call a cab if they had the cash.

"They're literally hostaged into having babies they can't or don't want to raise, and no police force in the state will acknowledge their plights, all predictably in hock to the whiphand of that shitbird Hawkwhip," Kay explained.

"Today we're freeing several women," she added as we crept half-bent across bone-dry mud towards the least-observed portion of the compound, where a mole in the security detail had been lavishly bribed into helping escort women toward the undergrowth where they could scarper unseen. Crouching by a flimsy bush below a hole in the mesh fence, we kept hush under the friction of cicadas and rumble of the highway, waiting for the bribed mole to observe the torch signal beaming from our torch to his head. Once observed, he returned two flickers to indicate the release was imminent and to ready our legs for scarpering. The situation exploded. Suddenly, three pregnant women were waddle-zooming our way, hurling themselves through the fence and barely stopping for breath as we crouch-sprinted to the escape car and powered off along a series of B-roads and non-roads, avoiding a potential highway ambush in the event of CCTV detection.

The three escapees were harried and sickly-looking women at the upper limit of their termination windows. Kay provided them with water, sandwiches, and warm words of solidarity, spitting venom at the psycho kidnappers while speeding them to their pre-booked appointments at the Sulphur City Abortion Centre, only several hours east. Later I spoke to Kim Schwartz, who had been unable to talk in the back of the land cruiser. She shed light on the stranger things that went on inside the compound. "Our bellies were attached to an ultrasound for an hour every evening. A flock of craven religious nuts would crowd round our beds and fall to their knees before the foetus on the screen before them and say a prayer. They appeared struck with reverent awe for this unformed agglomeration of cells twitchily forming in our bellies."

"These ceremonial hour-long sessions took place across the entirety of each prisoner's pregnancy," she continued, "as part of a Pro-Life package tour arranged by the Fifth Reformist Evangelical Church of the Sacred Jesuits of the Holy Womb of Christ of South Texas, whipping themselves into frenzies of pious fervour at sight of these foetuses twitching vaguely inside our amniotic sacs, as local pastors performed 2x-speed sermons in babel like glitching auctioneers. When our foetuses shed their cellular state to become born babies, the tours would applaud the empty ultrasounds, thank their hosts, and leave without so much as peeping at the newborn babies crying in their mothers' arms. In fact, several people requested that the noisy, crying brats were removed so they could soundlessly reflect on the miracle of the foetus on the screen vanishing into life. We were permitted several hours to rest then strongarmed in a state of exhaustion by our armed captors to the highway outside the compound to commence our motherly duties, assuming we managed to stagger home or hitch a ride. Several mothers, having spiralled into psychosis in their stay, left their babies on the side of the road and wandered into the desert to perish in the hellish Texas heat. The babies, too, were usually left to perish on the roadside, unless a kindly driver came to the rescue. These warped people are more interested in the antenatal and the afterlife than actual life itself. They spend their stupid lives in a state of fury at anyone who wishes to spend their brief time on this planet pursuing anything approximating happiness."

Kay accompanied the women inside the clinic, providing life-saving support as they moved from one trauma to the next. Her rescue package included staying with them at a motel for several days. "It's better they lie low," she said to me, leading the women to their rooms at the Easy Sleep Motel. "News of their escape will be all over social media. People become bored if there is no sighting of the escapees within two days, allowing our women to return home to their normal lives unmolested. We recommend they check regularly for any signs the local militia may be creeping around their homes. Several properties have been firebombed by extremists in the past."

Most women are relieved after their procedures. "Any reluctance we may have felt at having our abortions vanished the minute we were abducted," Kim told me. "Killing a foetus causes these sickos more agony than a mass shooting involving their own kids. To cause these mindless religious thugs acute trauma by taking control of our own bodies is the only crumb of comfort we can take from the whole fucking nightmare." One of the three women I met who wishes to remain anonymous explained that some victims, having birthed their babies under duress, made a point of tracking down the local pastors and placing their unwanted children on their doorsteps. Unfortunately, as a form of revenge, this is useless, as the kids only end up in the local orphanage, a place run by religious zealots. The perfect breeding ground for hard-right nutcases who kidnap women.

Moving on from Kay and the brave women kind enough to share their stories with me, I returned to Texas for a far more terrifying encounter. This involved terrorist troll faction The Libtrigger Boys, whose antics had taken root in Texas two years into Trump's presidency. Taking their lead from their tangerine führer, their MO was to perform illiberal stunts to cause terminal conniptions in the souls of the woke left. They had recently live-streamed a mass school shooting on Facebook in response to recent attempts by Democratic congressman Coky Warden to restrict the sale of Kalashnikovs to the under fives. A banner on their stream read THE 2ND AMENDMENT IS A SACRED RIGHT as the shooters went from class to class executing teachers and children with the perfunctory steeliness of movie assassins. Upon completion of their patriotic massacre, the organiser said to camera: "What you're seeing here is maybe your own kid lying in a pool of blood. Maybe this is your brother or sister. Your response is probably one of horror and repulsion. But you must ask yourself, patriots, what's more important, your right to bear arms and protect our inviolate second amendment, or your child's temporary existence? You can always have more kids, my friends. If we lose our right to bear arms in the United States, that's a precious right we'll never have back. These brave patriots died here today to show you the importance in which we hold the second amendment and that we must sacrifice our lives or other people's lives to protect our freedoms. Whether you're defending your home from intruders, hunting caribou in the wild, or conducting a mass school shooting because mean bitches on TikTok made you feel like a pussy, you should always have the right to feel a cool piece of metal in your hand as a true patriotic American. God bless you, kind folks, and God bless this country."

America's motto is *e pluribus unum* (translated: yesterday's mass school shooting is yesterday's news). The non-stop 24-hour newsgasm of our post-2016 world moves at breakneck speed, from a politician smuggling heroin in his mistress's anus, to a KKK militia furious at liberals who refuse to have a sensible conversation about race in this country, to a multi-state sequence of simultaneous school shootings live-streamed in 4K HD on Facebook. Garnering huge support from Texas lawmakers, The Libtrigger Boys were never prosecuted for their massacres. Even worse, schools started writing to The Boys to request their "gun-ho" appearance at their schools to help with crowd-funding social media campaigns (funds raised sent straight to the NRA), promising kids they too may have the lucky opportunity to spill their blood and innards to protect the 2nd amendment. These live-streamed shootings became commonplace for patriotic headteachers eager to show their allegiance to the stars and stripes. The image of a schoolchild's blasted head with his brain splatted across an American flag became an enduring source of pride for all God-fearing Texan patriots.

I met Sam Trader in a Waco diner. A world-weary, mustachioed park ranger in his late fifties, Sam led a band of well-armed liberals who used the Boys' own philosophy to reduce their spread and influence.

"There are thousands of people in this state who think our children's brains shouldn't be used as propaganda for Trumpian wingnuts," he said, sipping a water. He took long pauses, savouring the relative calm of the moment. He described The Boys' latest wheeze, to force orthodox Muslim women into clearings and have them strip naked. Streaming their tearful undressings on Facebook, the Boys would make "encouraging" comments on their bodies. "American women are proud to show off their legs, their asses, their titties. They don't hide themselves under black robes. The bikini is the official uniform of every woman in this here US of A." They would then proceed to masturbate on the women while praying then release them in their underwear.

"They think it's clever to cause libtard meltdowns, and claim they want to bring about a mass exodus of Democrats," Sam said. "They have a separate mob on the Mexico border, where they set up large trebuchets, placing immigrant families inside and launching them across the country, where they meet their sticky end against rocks. I formed our resistance organisation Men from the Boys in opposition to these psychobozos. They've become a lawless militia in the state backed up by our corrupt cops and politicians, free to execute anyone they feel is against their moronic lib-baiting agenda." Similar second amendment-loving folks who resented their kids being murdered, Men from the Boys took up arms and began hunting down members of the Boys, live-streaming their executions on Facebook.

"The right to bear arms includes the right to seek justice for those who murder our children," Sam said. His implacable logic cemented the group's popularity among grieving parents who had quietly craved revenge for their losses, or those too terrified to speak out against this SS-esque militia.

It was tacitly accepted by the monumentally thick Texas law enforcement that if folks were allowed to conduct mass shootings of school children in the name of protecting the second amendment, then it stood to reason that folks could in turn shoot the shooters in the name of the second amendment. I asked Sam if he was worried this logic might result in a stream of revenge killings for revenge killings ad nauseam, but he wasn't worried. "Most folk approve of our executions. We received two hundred superchats on YouTube when we executed the killer of twenty kids at Hubbard Elementary School last week," he said. His dolorous delivery, his yard-long stare, his teary eyes, made me very depressed. I thanked him for his time and headed west of Waco.

My West Texas was a paradise/hell of blood-orange skies over austere curves and peaks, sprawling desert flats bereft of bison or any wildlife, and lonesome highways custom made for Willie Nelson karaoke atrocities. My primary fear was that a mercenary Corvette of hoodlums would rear-end me off-road and perform inventive acts of torture on my eyes in a conveniently adjacent barn. My secondary fear was that a police car stopped me speeding and hauled me over the bumper of my car, blackening my skin with face paint so they could shoot me in the head with impunity. My tertiary fear was that the sun burned a whole in my bumper, setting my engine ablaze, forcing me to stagger through the desert pursued by scorpions and vultures until I accidentally stumbled into a Native-American reservation and was made to apologise for my ancestors introducing Europeans to the Americas in the first place. None of these fears were realised.

I arrived in the desert city of Marfa, an arty haven named after two erotic dramas by Larry Clark, to meet Dr. Bill Waxter. Late for our meeting at the funky Frama coffeehouse, I parlayed with a lawyer for the firm Venn & Penhurst who represented local politicians and broadcasters. He informed me of the trend in American politics to call anyone with whom you disagreed politically a paedophile. This phenomenon started when batty congresswoman Carly Brown Bilge called her competitor in the senate race a "foetus-killing gun-hating paedophile socialist". The technique, in the pre-Trump era, was to accuse your left-wing opponent of loving abortions, of writhing around in pools of aborted foetuses, and to show videos of defenceless (white) suburbanites unable to protect their property from hordes of (black) burglars and rapists. Times had changed, to paraphrase America's bard.

Brown Bilge popularised the tactic of labelling all nemeses paedophiles. An eruption of lawsuits sprung up in the wake of this surge of paedophile accusations from prominent politicians. Newscasters on Fox reported the news in a manner like: "Paedophile Democrat Andrew Yang spoke to a mob of paedophile Democrat supporters in Houston today. This is the second visit by paedophile Presidential Candidate Yang, and the sixth visit from a paedophile Democrat in the last two weeks. It's important for these paedophile senators to appeal to their paedophile base, while the rest of us hardworking Americans carry on being patriots and not paedophiles and voting Republican."

"These lawsuits are manna for us," this lawyer said. "If we're clever, we can Jarndyce these mothers for years and years, as our opponents tend to produce doctored photos or pay for testimonials attesting to the paedophilic nature of the people they are calling paedophiles. Their technique, I suppose, is to have the word 'paedophile' associated with their enemy for as long as possible regardless of the truth, and more broadly to redefine 'paedophile' as a synonym for liberal or Democrat. The electoral damage is already done, and the accusers are usually elected politicians by the time the lawsuits end and can easily use taxpayers' money to pay their settlements."

"What a country," I said.

"You're very welcome here," he said, skipping to his car.

Dr. Waxler arrived an hour late, a sudden sexual encounter with his secretary Barbara Brockhaus his stated reason. He asked me to refrain from describing his appearance, preferring to remain anon for the nonce.

"She's a cosmo ho," he said, shaking my British mitt.

"I see."

"How'd you find my chill pill?"

"I mellowed pretty sharpish upon popping," I said. "My shanks reclined to an optimum level of cool and I had no paranoid visions of souljacking as the plane taxied to rest in the Houston dusk."

"Yes'm. I've had feederback from folks who said their souls never arose from their bodies into nimbuses of strait."

"You may be on to something."

"Yessir. I want to talk to you today about my new'un. You may've read my astute piece on the use of remdesivir in halting athlete's foot while bathing in untreated water. Well, in the lab last week I magicked aloft twelve particles of that sweet medicine to a new compound, TYP^0. No, that ain't no spelling mistake! Preliminary testing of my new comp revealed that upon taking two puffs an hour, Democrats shed more and moreso of their liberalism and very speedily turned Republican. If I can refine this form-you-lie, you're lookin' at the hottest poh-little-cull proper-tee on the planet here'm," he said, becoming more Texan in syntax as his enthusiasm upped.

"Hmm, I observe flaws in this drug," I said. "If everyone turns Republican, the entire country will be infected with the madness of Texas. Electing untalented carpetbaggers with paltry oratory skills to positions of high office will only lead to the complete unravelling of every institution in the land and a breakdown of order and a swift plunge into a state of lawless chaos where the populace compete to bag the most human kills while nibbling on untasty muskrats."

"Isn't that where we're heading anyway? My drug you could say is an accelerant of the inevitable."

"I wouldn't use that in the advertising."

"Yes. There's also the threat that an imbalance in my compound's fizzies may cause people to politically haemorrhage and vote for the Swan Uppers or the Stalinists. This will require more consideration."

"Thanks for my pills, Doc."

"You're welcome. By the way, watch out for visions of Mary Steenburgen on a plinth. Some users of my chill pill have reported that issue."

"I will."

As I waved howdy-bye to the pretty parchlands of the rural and the sweaty honk of the urban, I reflected upon my experiences with the abortion Ubers, the executors of mass shooters, and the peculiar lawyers and doctors making their plays in the land of plays. It was apparent that America had become intellectually clotted in the faulty vesicle of its own mythology. The spirit of eccentricity that had seen the country bloat phenomenally from the brutality of slavery to the jackhammer pep of modernism, from the illusory convection of creativity and commerce in the booming 1960s to the carefully coordinated creation of a class of superrich autocrats who buy and sell democracy, had long departed. Cutthroat capitalism has turned America into a feudal hellhole, where mindless parasites rally round ultra-rich amoral psychopaths making secret plans to retreat to Mars once the planet they have comprehensively fucked burns to a crispy, cinder-black mass, hoping to osmotically save themselves from violent death by the sheer force of their hero-worship.

The kooky Golden Age eccentricities of the flappers, the rockers, the hippies *et al* have rotted in time and turned poisonous. American eccentricity is now inseparable from political extremism. The kooky is now the KKKooky. As ordinary Americans waved their pompoms for unregulated capitalism, they have seen the triumph of their wonderful country slowly ebbed raw by ruthless, cash-hoovering media moguls, pitting ordinary people against each other every night on national TV by paid hatemongers using their phoney patriotism as an electoral cattleprod. Make America Great is the Five Minutes Hate.

America, a country in freefall.

Americans in America hollering at other Americans in America that they are unamerican traitors to America for making the slightest criticism of anything remotely American. A country utterly unable and unwilling to examine itself. Utterly unable to reconcile itself with its violent and racist past. Utterly unable to temper the philosophy of spectacular greed and lust for power, a nightmare cunningly concealed as a dream. Utterly unwilling to recognise reality. Utterly enmeshed in the decrees of an ancient constitution. Sunk by the veneration of ignorance and idiocy, a country where the thickest loons are rewarded for their thickness, with a public too thick to realise how thick they are for electing thick loons to rule over them. A place of promise, hope, and possibility, reduced to a bleeding haemorrhoid of lying news anchors, lying politicians, lying multi-millionaires, with no vision beyond heaping manna upon manna in pursuit of immortality.

A country lorded over by narcissistic billionaires, emotionally bankrupt men who use their vast fortunes not to reshape the planet into a habitable place for the poorest and the neediest, but to construct spaceships to enhance their coolness rating one above Bruce Willis. A country so raped and ruined by greed and self-interest no one can pause for a second without the ravenous hogs of debt, despair, desolation, and dementia chewing them to pieces. A country raving madly in the asylum attic, spooking away the bats. A babbling, incoherent wreck with bloody swastikas carved in its face, squatting on the White House lawn in piss-stained cords hurling turds at the moon.

These were my thoughts as Mary Steenburgen sat unblinking on a plinth several lightyears away, her creepy Botoxed face making my skin crawl. So howdy-bye, America. I hope y'all can afford the therapy.

Mike Silverton

Trios

All at sea in anomie? Wondering what it's
all about? Install an arm
ature.

Stardust fashions impressions with unreliable fingers.
Debris clutters unregistered canyons.
Cadence marks time.

Certain afflictions simply are. Certain
attractions include me
teors.

Snakes of more than ordinary rarity dwell among mongooses,
in the main, stealthily. Fact: hedgehogs are
stupid.

Of no particular discernment, mayhem (including defenestration) operates
under canopies, in arenas and, why
not, ogre patios.

I won't dance, you can't make me. I also won't bark.
And I wish to remind that magicians
are people.

Disregard questionable emotions. Be amiable. Jockey for a favorable
outcome. Pause to consider
décor.

Inquiry is especially fruitful in divination by turds. While it's true I've just
spoken, I will soon eat my words. Am busy
assorting condiments.

The optimist's daughters are largely stationery. But when they step out
in their perfect slippers golden coupons spring up from
the earth.

If one submits himself to a branch chipper could we call it chop
suicide, or would that sound too much
like food?

Spend your days aloft with a latex-free familiar. Place
your legs in God's hands and turn on
the shaking alarm.

Bedside assistants and swimming-pool golf await the faithful. And
jumbo thermometers. Mounting brackets
included.

Recent additions include a nose-hair stimulant, a Krakatoa
replica, irresolute geese and non-fungible
mists.

Your large, creamy white head turns pink as
the night grows cooler and
slices easily.

Create a maze. Stuff with piñatas. Bombard with bowling balls,
rocks, paper weights, whatever's handy,
take notes.

Kick back, unwind, entertain the Onanist Clique with cautionary
maxims. "Idle hands are playthings . . .",
and so on.

While I wouldn't call myself a cook, I can't stop. I poached my hand
overnight, I mean Friday night, and the kids
didn't smell a thing.

My memories taste like pipe cleaners. Autumn
leaves and dollops occupy the
slots.

"Sutures!" she cried, floating across the moors. "Or something else!"
Snowflakes, I'm writing little poems on all of you
today.

And that's not all, I said, and jumped up and down. Thank you! Next!
Hey, droopy drawers, upon my boughs the birds,
they don't loiter.

Addressing the dark as Shady Joe is visionary enough but
certainly not as tasty as nostalgia
in aspic.

Literati swoon at the thought of a sestina and who's
been riding a bicycle in
here?

The poet has an eel by the tail. If not quite true,
it is at least clearly stat
ed.

Hi, Betty. Hi, Martha. How about that Grand Vizier,
whacking the Madonna around like
that?

Permit me to donate to your complacence. Ethnicity
is entirely felicitous, like fart bubbles
in the bath.

To the sentient tablecloth the dining room ceiling is heaven. An
ominous passerby bursts in on the dinner party
and spills wine.

Deciduous police all have wide eyes and some have tiny hearing aids.
And sparrow feathers in their chapeaux. They avoid
sunlight.

You cannot fully appreciate digestion until
you've walked barefoot in
shit.

Something gray lies somewhere ahead. And thin-
soup manifestos. And distant coups
d'etoile.

For further study: the muted pings of eyelid
collision, an encrypted meatball's
putrefaction.

 Digame, hombre, where are the snoods? The viaducts, gone, the temples,
gone, and as I just learned, passion subsides
at room temperature.

Vers spasmodique resembles carrots flying out doors. I, meanwhile, board
Airship Destiny perchance to an epiphany, and lo, there goes
Popeye in a petal-fragrant sky.

Drop everything. Fine-tune your vision. Calibrate your hearing.
Savor the universe in a dozen days
or less.

Commodore Perry issues three suggestions: avoid waste,
observe equanimity, queen among postures,
and remain perpendicular.

We've plenty of feet to carry us there. Carious? Where?
You're probably wondering, who is
this alarmist?

Lady Murasaki pitches cherry-blossom pies
At narcoleptic ronin striking
yam-like poses.

Pensées, permafrost, walnuts.
Aim nozzle at sky and
squeeze.

Astride a monument, Respighi
lectures in disheveled
triplicate.

Poetry recommends sniffing teargas
the better to grasp the
Zeitgeist.

A broken tooth in a pasta primavera? A bent fork in
a tiramisu? Is that even likely?
No!

There exist turns of speech which, if not quite metaphors,
are sufficiently allusive to require
curiosity.

Hélas! Hoopla! Zut! How akin to wandering,
the heart, it sees and flutters.
Urrk!

A puff of air costumed as nothingness installs desire
in a cadaver. The morgue becomes
a tourist attraction.

Observing vistas through dainty pink toes. Poetry!
From pillar to post to any
where!

I call her Electricidad on Wednesdays. On weekends,
Zephyr. As an endearment, Little
Snotfish.

The poet notes a viper's proximity and – pop! pop! pop! –
breaks out in logorrhea. It proves oddly
effective.

Many canaries live in cages. Most buzzards do not.
And there lies a sand dollar, alone
and wistful.

One makes the best of limping and
leaking on his way to a
crevasse.

Dogs acquire ticks by chance. As for me,
I'm sailing to Capri via
trebuchet.

I'm prepared to say a word about ambidexterity as
soon as you tell me why your eyeballs
do that thing.

Pseudopods stride across dunes assembled
from a/c filters and virgins'
navels.

Find me a nice obelisk. Plant me on top. I'll be
ornamental, like a flesh-tone
stove pipe.

All within sight and beyond, refurbished. The galaxies
are singing Bring Us Some More
in four-part harmony.

"The sound unuttered lives deep within the breast." Flat-faced
from chastisement with cast-iron skillets ought
at least to warrant an ouch.

Selective breeding has me here, fishing with
Little Willy. A nibble only.
Sigh.

A motif is like a dollhouse. It's not
useful when you can't
see it.

And now, Melpomene, Poetry celebrates
a denouement, insomnia and
dental hygiene.

Musical clams are inapposite. Snow White's acne is
inapposite. Supplementation with vitamins is
often unnecessary.

Tomoé Hill

The Dress and The Bench

In Siena there is a column at the edge of the old city: on it, a statue of Romulus and Remus with the she-wolf. Legend says when Senius and his brother Aschius—founders of Siena and the sons of Remus—fled Rome, the pair took with them the wolf as a reminder of their origin. You would not call me a seasoned traveller or nomad; to be honest, and not least of all to myself, I am the sort of person for whom travelling is escape—not in a romantic sense, but to flee. It does not mean bare survival, as we bear witness to in the news every day, but nevertheless closer to that in its small way than anything else. Survival simply means to be able to continue to exist, and there have been times where it has been nec-essary to try find a way back to a recognisable existence or take the opportunities which presented themselves, despite not knowing where they would lead or how I would find myself—if at all—once there.

Continuation is never equal to certainty or contentment, and its assurances are so minimal that at some point we seek to embellish our presence with meanings we glean from wherever we are. It serves as a reminder that narratives are found—or find us—as much as they are created, and as Henry Miller, writing about Big Sur says in *Big Sur and the Oranges of Hieronymus Bosch*, 'one's destination is never a place but rather a new way of looking at things. Which is to say there are no limits of vision'. It is when we stop being able to see that a sense of restlessness or even fear comes over us; maybe this is in some way a primal remnant, but it is nevertheless a sense worth heeding, for it propels us towards an unknown which is necessary to who it is we eventually become, that process of becoming nothing more than another kind of journey. I had lost this sight not once or twice but three times in my life so far, each loss resulting in another relocation. It was in this way I found myself in Italy, not far from Siena.

I am a terrible tourist. In a new place, I find myself wishing the streets and buildings and faces were already committed to memory. Instead of the sharp angular motions of a head and neck turning to glimpse a street sign, I long for the grace of intuitive recognition, the almost imperceptible glance and nod of familiarity. The stride of those well-acquainted with a place is unbroken, except to stop and converse with others who are the same. Their feet know the stones and pavements below them so well that there is no need to look down at the path they take. The tourist is akin to a newborn foal: all awkward limbs and head, attempting to walk, stand, and speak in an unfamiliar tongue all at once, failing. If I longed for Miller's new way of looking, then I also wanted its period of adjustment to be over, to settle into it with the pleasure of knowing I no longer had to account for my newness within that perception. Slowly, through a kind of osmosis, what the mind maps the body translates in its movements. This knowledge, once attained, never leaves, and even now I find myself able to mimic walking the gradual incline along the city wall near the statue, or one of the uneven sets of steps that lead down to the Piazza del Campo, replicating alongside them the scents of almond biscuits or the savoury coriander and anise of cavallucci, 'little horses'; the by turns warm and acrid sharply violet leather drifting from open doorways whose insides displayed shelves of bags and layers of belts hanging like austere streamers; the fatty smell of chunks of soppressata flecked with nutmeg; real cigarette smoke always paired with fresh, bitterly dark espresso, the fumes of vice and necessity entwined.

There was a boutique I would stop and look into each time we came to the city; the cobbled street it was on was part of the sloping walk in from where we would park. Curiously, it was rarely open which made it feel all the more like a message from a dream. For months, a dress was on display in the window. A simple utilitarian shirtdress, it was knee-length, long-sleeved, and tied at the waist, but made of luxuriously heavy olive green silk which had the dull sheen of a mirror's gilt worn by time. Priced at few hundred euros, I coveted the dress for almost six months but never bought it. It would have been a special purchase, but even then I could not seem to justify it. Running around a rambling property chopping and stacking wood, gathering wild herbs, aware that there were errant scorpions and spiders, I wore only practical garments which would bear the burrs and marks of such a life: to wear beautiful things meant to be stained with the juice and colours of the surrounding nature, painted by necessity.

The dress reminded me of an article I read in an obscure magazine at about age eleven or twelve. This could be one of those misremembered memories, but I remember it being called *Almanac*, something we received because my parents had a book subscription which consisted of monthly receipts of leather-bound gilt-edged classics such as *Lolita* and *Winesburg, Ohio*. For such an unheard-of publication, *Almanac* had extraordinary pretensions to the megalith glossy lifestyle and fashion magazines like *Vogue* and *Architectural Digest*. Issues were full of Absolut Vodka ads at their apogee; there were multi-page layouts of models in bold and vibrant Christian Lacroix outfits complete with hats clashing brilliantly against zebra banquettes in the reopened El Morocco nightclub; model-less but no less fashionable shoots featuring lamps of increasingly abstract designs titled LIGHT—an unsubtle declaration that even divine creation could benefit from a glamorous update. I would carefully tear them out and tape them inside my school locker, for some time unaware that teachers and students alike would double-take upon realising they weren't inspirational posters or ones of pop stars.

Even then, I dreamt of a certain escape which I felt could be achieved through materiality; an object which would conjure a narrative beyond my Midwestern one, transforming me into something I could not imagine but nevertheless desired. That spark of unknown desire functions like a garment: in our lives we try many on, and unless intuitively versed in the language of fashion, often not realising until our later years that it is not just any one which will suit who we are. We will become struck by an abundance of both desires and clothes, trying them on and mostly discarding them, until we find the ones which we feel we have known or worn forever, though they may only fit us during a certain time in our lives. Upon understanding this, you also come to know the seasonality of desire. The necessity of allowing them to sleep and wake, to wither and bloom as if they were fruit, flowers, or as simple as animals; a destiny out of our hands, in those of something greater.

Besides these features, there were pieces written by what I now imagine were up-and-coming writers, although I no longer remember their names. A single article has remained in my memory—about regret, specifically of a purchase never made. For some weeks the author had gone to an antique shop, each time lingering inside over an old cobbler's bench. She could not understand the attraction but always found herself hesitating over it, touching the old wood, the proprietor urging her to sit and get a feel for it. She loved that bench with the unrealised love of someone who does not yet grasp how objects can shape their outlook of the world, who still bends to the

idea that one must love certain things at certain times, as if in doing so they had the ability to solidify the narrative of who they thought they must be. I cannot recall the price beyond it being the exact amount of a pair of heels that she bought instead; beautiful uncomfortable shoes which hurt her. Worn to a few parties and richly complimented, they only reminded her of the old bench of her unknown desire, since sold. All that remained of her folly were aching feet, useless shoes, and the chapter in *Little Women* (which she was reading), 'Meg Goes to Vanity Fair', where the eldest daughter, naïve of the small manipulations and machinations that fuel society, allows herself to be elaborately dressed and made up for a party, so unlike herself that she spends the evening regretting that she had not stayed true to her simpler self.

The desire for the bench was never articulated, though retrospectively she must have known precisely what it symbolised: the means to dream and create. Like Woolf's room of one's own, more compactly realised. But her beautiful shoes were another kind of lesson: though we may regret certain desires, they are no less important in their failure as well as their timing. It is simplicity itself to assume the narrative of one's life follows only the easiest path, especially being reared as we are in such material surroundings. But our reality is very much that of recognising we are not the person we wished to be: that it is not possible to become with only a pair of shoes or a dress, and the tools of transformation are often mundane, invisible, even ugly to the unknowing. One does not question the purpose of the butterfly's cocoon but we are sometimes unable to see the forms of our own cocoons, instead taking on the coloured mantle and wings too early. It is not that wisdom is drab, but unremarkable to the eye until we adjust the palette of our sight.

As much as I longed for the dress, I knew it would be of as much use as the writer's heels.

What use was its beautiful heavy silk, folds so out of place amidst the tangles of rosemary and spiderwebs which laced and embroidered the old stones? What version of myself was I hoping to recall amidst the wildness of this new life? The dress was a ghost, and I too attached to the memories of a self similarly clad to be able to fully recognise that my desire was akin to a séance. My own representation of the author's bench—my cocoon—lay in the uninteresting but necessary purchases and everyday doings required of temporary rusticity: firewood, bags of wood-pulp pellets for heating, a new saw-blade, picking olives, looking at nothing and everything when I gazed into the valley whose edge the house perched. I was happy to embrace the simplicity, for the same reason I moved—to become part of it; the beautiful contradiction of knowing the solitude of belonging. That solitude yields what Miller again refers to as 'the fullness and richness of life . . . in simplifying our lives, everything acquires a significance hitherto unknown'. One realises that new way of seeing is simply for it is always simple when finally achieved—the result of a harmony between the internal and external. That Miller was right when he said it was not a matter of place but of perception, the ability to find and keep hold of it regardless of location. The precariousness and unease of continuation suddenly finds its stillness; the traveller is finally home.

In order to attain that becoming and vision in another culture, you live fully as those around you, sharing a dream of familiar objects and seasons; a cobbler's bench for a community. We lived as they lived, following the clock of the earth, marking time with the last golden grapes which were the sunset of fall, then the sunrise of the citrus fruits of winter. To appreciate this bounty, you must for a while forget the summer fruits which came before, allowing them to reside in nothing but a distant memory of hope. They will come

again, or perhaps not—this is what it means to live in and with time, its little deaths and rebirths. Though Miller uses Hieronymus Bosch's oranges to illustrate the ideal of perception, to me it is Francisco de Zubarán's still lifes that capture the sense of my own newfound sight. His lemons, grapes, quinces, and melons, set against a black background seem to exist in a state of reflection. They do not have the vivid tones of reality despite appearing real, instead taking on the sheen of that silk dress; slightly tarnished, as if from the edges of a dream. They are present, but the black creeping ever closer to the foreground serves to remind us that their absence is never far off, a shroud that only enriches the cycle of possessing and not. Colour decomposes to black which eventually yields colour once again, a trust not dissimilar to the abyss of sleep.

What one remembers most of all is time itself is an unseen, unrealised desire. It is the ones who live under the veil of illness or a very threat to their survival who understand they are the fruits in such a painting. Here, I understood what it was to keep time and live with it, each second a conscious breath. It struck me that this form of timekeeping was non-existent in my former city. Rejecting the chronology of nature, it was instead a state of perpetual, artificial bloom in which it became impossible to both mourn and look forward. Instead of black, there was a blinding white which cast no light nor sense of life. And so I finally realised that I, too, had to shed my former existence: each time we went to Siena, I would linger for a moment or two at the shop window, admiring the dress which would have been more appropriate for my past in London. Without regret, I would then move on to the shops and stalls supplying the dream-washed moments which formed the meaning of my Italian present.

JACK FOLEY

SOME WORDS ABOUT WILLIAM BUTLER YEATS

FOR ANGELA MANLY

"As I look backward upon my own writing, I take pleasure alone in those verses where it seems to me I have found something hard and cold, some articulation of the Image which is the opposite of all that I am in my daily life, and all that my country is; yet man or nation can no more make this Mask or Image than the seed can be made by the soil into which it is cast."

    —William Butler Yeats, "Hodos Chameliontos," "The Path of the Chameleon" (1922)

"We who care deeply about the arts find ourselves the priesthood of an almost forgotten faith, and we must, I think, if we would win the people again, take upon ourselves the method and the fervour of a priesthood . . . We must baptize as well as preach."

    —William Butler Yeats, "Ireland and the Arts" (1901)

"We Irish, born into that ancient sect,
But thrown upon this filthy modern tide,
And by its formless spawning fury wrecked,
Climb to our proper dark, that we may trace
The lineaments of a plummet-measured face."

    —William Butler Yeats, "The Statues" (1938)

"I have found in an old diary a quotation from Stephane Mallarmé, saying that his epoch was troubled by the trembling of the veil of the Temple."

    —William Butler Yeats, *The Trembling of the Veil* (1922)

I've written (and published) a couple of papers about Yeats, one of my master poets. I believe that the "official" interpretations of several of his poems are inaccurate. "Among School Children" and "The Second Coming" are spectacularly so. Yeats was an esoteric poet: there are things you need to know—things you need to be privy to—when you encounter his poems.

As Paul de Man was the first to notice, shining through Yeats' naturalistic "imagery" is a notion expounded by the Neoplatonist, Porphyry (232/3 – ca. 305) in his *De Antro Nympharum*, a commentary on the Cave of the Nymphs episode in *The Odyssey*. Yeats knew Porphyry's essay through Thomas Taylor's once widely-read translation, and he refers explicitly to it in the footnote about "the drug" in "Among School Children." More importantly, he also quotes extensively from the essay in "The Philosophy of Shelley's Poetry"—one of the pieces collected in *Ideas of Good and Evil* (1903)—and there are unmistakable references to Porphyry in both Blake and Spenser as well as in Yeats' own work. Appearing in *The Witch of Atlas*, *The Book of Thel*, and in the third Book of *The Faerie Queene*, the cluster of symbols discussed in Porphyry's essay is one of the key items of literary Neoplatonism.

As described by Porphyry, the Cave of the Nymphs is a kind of half-way house for all souls about to be born or about to ascend to heaven; as such it is regarded as the source of all life, which is symbolized by "waters welling everywhere." One of its gates—"the gate of generation"—leads to the earth, and the other—"the gate of ascent through death to the gods"—leads to heaven. The first is "the gate of cold and moisture," for "cold...causes life in the world," and the second is "the gate of heat and fire." If we keep only these details in mind—and Porphyry goes on to add a great many others—we can see how the Cave of the Nymphs is relevant to a poem like "The Wild Swans at Coole." The "brimming water among the stones" is Yeats' equivalent to the water welling among the rocks of the cave, and the two activities of the swans—"They paddle in the cold / Companionable streams or climb the air"—represent respectively the descent of the soul into matter through the gate of cold and moisture and, since air is a purer element than water, the ascent to the divine. Yeats often imagines this ascent as proceeding in "rings" or "gyres" (the swans "scatter wheeling in great broken rings") and as accompanied by the sound of a bell, here, "the bell-beat of their wings above my head." (Cf. the bells in "Byzantium" and "All Souls' Night.") The association of swans—and birds generally—with souls is an important trope in Yeats' work:

> Some moralist or mythological poet
> Compares the solitary soul to a swan;
> I am satisfied with that . . .

There are many ways in which Porphyry influences Yeats. And it is important to know that the two gates are always a unitary phenomenon: where the one gate is, the other is as well: "They paddle in the cold / Companionable streams or climb the air."

Indeed, many of Yeats' poems change their meanings once we allow for the presence of Porphyry and other esoteric elements. I mentioned that the two gates are a unitary phenomenon. In Yeats' famous poem, "The Second Coming," everything in the entire opening passage is usually taken to mean more or less the same thing.

> Turning and turning in the widening gyre,
> The falcon cannot hear the falconer;
> Things fall apart; the center cannot hold;
> Mere anarchy is loosed upon the world,
> etc.

In most interpretations, the falcon's inability to hear the falconer is parallel to things falling apart: it is another example of "anarchy": an image of chaos.

Perhaps.

But note the concluding lines: "And what rough beast, its hour come round at last / Slouches towards Bethlehem to be born?" Being born is the gate of generation. Where then is the other gate, "the gate of ascent"?

> Turning and turning in the widening gyre,
> The falcon cannot hear the falconer . . .

The opening lines are *not* an image of chaos: they are an image of *escape*. The falconer is trying to lure the falcon back to the earth, where everything is falling apart. The falcon is escaping from all that and moving towards the divine: "They paddle in the cold, / Companionable streams or *climb the air*." It is the only moment in the poem where Yeats offers us an alternative to the way of the beast.

That Yeats allows his reader to misunderstand the opening lines is part of why we must regard him as an *esoteric* writer. If you have been through the proper initiation, if you know your Porphyry, for example, you may understand him. For the ordinary reader, the poem is only about the horrors of the modern world. There is no indication of escape from those horrors.

Similarly, the conclusion of "Among School Children" is pretty much universally taken to be positive—about an ecstatic state in which you can't tell dancer from dance. As such, the line is understood to be a rhetorical question. But the whole burden of the poem is about distinctions, particularly the distinction between images: "Both nuns and mothers worship images, / But those the candle lights are not as those / That animate a mother's reveries." Two diametrically opposed kinds of images. A primary theme of the poem is Yeats' relationship to Maud Gonne: "She stands before me as a living child." The young Yeats took Maud Gonne's beauty to be an image of divine beauty—an image like those worshipped by nuns. As he looks at her in the now of the poem, she is anything but that: "Her present image floats into the mind, / Did Quattrocento finger fashion it? / Hollow of cheek as though it drank the wind / And took a mess of shadows for its meat." Her growing old and losing her beauty are clear indications that she is not the kind of "image" worshipped by nuns: she is the kind of "image" that animates a mother's reveries. Unlike the images worshipped by nuns, her beauty is not timeless but caught forever in time. Was the young Yeats' reaction to her the reaction of his soul, as he believed it to be, or was it his libido? The poem is a reluctant and oblique admission that it was the latter. The answer to the first of the poem's concluding questions, "O chestnut tree, great rooted blossomer, / Are you the leaf, the blossom or the bole?" is *No, it is not*. The "great rooted blossomer" is an image like those nuns worship; it is not the tree that exists in time: leaf and blossom are by definition temporal phenomena. Similarly, the second question, "O body swayed to music, O brightening glance, / How can we know the dancer from the dance?" is not a rhetorical question asserting the unity of dancer and dance but a genuine, anguished question. Yeats' failure to know the difference between dancer (nature) and dance (archetypal image) in the instance of his misplaced "worship" of Maud Gonne will certainly cost him time in Purgatory (cf. his play on that subject), may in fact cost him his soul. At one point he even insists that it is the artist's sad fate to have to "refuse / A heavenly mansion, raging in the dark":

> The intellect of man is forced to choose
> Perfection of the life, or of the work
> And if it take the second must refuse
> A heavenly mansion, raging in the dark.

I can quote further passages in support of what I'm saying here but this should give you an idea. "The Lake Isle of Innisfree" is also misinterpreted—it's full of images straight out of Porphyry—as is "A Dialogue of Self and Soul," which deals with the purgatorial process of living your whole life backwards, not with reincarnation, as is usually assumed. "Her Vision in the Wood" is a central poem in this mode of understanding. Quoting Porphyry's phrase, "fabulous symbol," the poem documents the particular "failure" at the heart of Yeats' enterprise. For the young Yeats, this phrase summed up his hopes not only for his own poetry but for the entire "symbolist" movement. The speaker of "Her Vision in the Wood" admits with horror that what she sees isn't a "fabulous symbol" at all but "my heart's victim and its torturer." Misplaced eros rather than transcendence. Libido rather than soul's love. How can we know the dancer from the dance?

> That thing all blood and mire, that beast-torn wreck,
> Half turned and fixed a glazing eye on mine,
> And, though love's bitter-sweet had all come back,
> Those bodies from a picture or a coin
> Nor saw my body fall nor heard it shriek,
> Nor knew, drunken with singing as with wine,
> That they had brought no fabulous symbol there
> But my heart's victim and its torturer.

. . .

"The Lake Isle of Innisfree" (1888)

In the recorded introductory remarks to a reading of the poem, Yeats explains that the name "Innisfree" means "Heather Island." He also asserts that the poem has only one "obscurity": when he writes of noon as "a purple glow," he is thinking of the reflection of the heather on the water. He goes on to tell us that the poem originated when he was in London: he was feeling homesick for his boyhood home, Sligo, and he saw an advertisement for "cooling drinks."

Despite Yeats' disclaimer, many of the details of the poem—the water, the honey, the bee and its hive, the color purple, the number nine, the beans—are from Porphyry. The "small cabin" is the poet's equivalent to the cave itself, which, he writes, "may mean any enclosed life, as when it is the dwelling place of Asia and Prometheus, or when it is 'the still cave of poetry.'" "Clay and wattles"—clay and sticks—I take to be flesh and bones, as when, in the much later poem, "Sailing to Byzantium," Yeats writes, "An aged man is but a paltry thing, / A tattered coat upon a stick . . ." Note also that "The Lake Isle of Innisfree" deliberately *deemphasizes* the visual—"veils of the morning," "purple glow," "glimmer"—but emphasizes the auditory: "bee-loud glade," "the cricket sings," "linnet's wings," "I hear lake water lapping," "low sounds." Indeed, the "sounds" referred to are in a way the "sounds" of the poem as we imagine it spoken—its wonderfully "musical" vowels and rhymes. Yeats was a great admirer of the scholar/critic Walter Pater, and a passage from Pater's *The Renaissance* (1873) may also be relevant here. Pater is writing of "music or musiclike intervals in our existence" and of "life itself . . . conceived as a sort of listening—listening to music . . . *to the sound of water*, to time as it flies. Often such moments are really our moments of play, and we are surprised at the unexpected blessedness" (my italics). There is of course also Pater's famous line, "All art constantly aspires toward the condition of music."

But Neoplatonism is not to be outdone by Estheticism. Plotinus's Fifth *Ennead* also emphasizes listening: "We must turn the perceptive faculty inward and hold it to attention there. Hoping to hear a desired voice, we let all others pass and are alert for the coming of that most welcome of sounds: so here, we must let the hearings of sense go by, save for sheer necessity, *and keep the soul's perception bright and quick to the sounds of above*" (my italics). I think as well that this passage from Yeats' "Hodos Chameliontos" elucidates what the poet means by "the deep heart's core," the central point from which everything emerges: "I know now that revelation is from the self, but from that age-long memoried self, that shapes the elaborate shell of the mollusc and the child in the womb, that teaches the birds to make their nest;

and that genius is a crisis that joins that buried self for certain moments to our trivial daily mind."

Such passages are relevant to the poem, whatever its connection to Yeats' childhood. I think the cricket, the linnet and the heather are indeed from the poet's childhood—from Innisfree itself—whereas other objects have esoteric resonances. Yeats is attempting to balance natural elements with supernatural ones. "Homesickness" is certainly an element of the poem, but so is the desire to turn homesickness into the longing for the divine. The situation here is similar to that in "The Wild Swans at Coole." For the young Yeats, the poet can transform landscape into "fabulous symbol." I noted earlier that that phrase, from Porphyry—"neither did the ancients establish temples without fabulous symbols"— appears in the lines quoted from "Her Vision in the Wood." In his early work Yeats was attempting to be Homer, to write the kind of poetry described in Porphyry's essay, "obscurely" indicating "the images of things of a more divine nature in the fiction of a fable." Even beyond this, Yeats' careful invocation of phrases and concepts from Porphyry's essay allows the poet to pretend that he can transform landscape into emblem. As such, the poem is an act of magic. By the time Yeats writes "Her Vision in the Wood" he understands his poetry in a very different way. "What can I but enumerate old themes?" he asks in a famous late poem, "The Circus Animals' Desertion":

> First that sea-rider Oisin led by the nose
> Through three enchanted islands, allegorical dreams . . .
> But what cared I that set him on to ride,
> I, starved for the bosom of his faery bride?

"Her Vision in the Wood" marks, at least momentarily, the total collapse of Yeats' enterprise. The attempt to transform landscape into "fabulous symbol"—and Maud Gonne into Leda—has failed entirely. Archetype remains but it remains separate from the poet's attempt to merge with it:

Both nuns and mothers worship images,
But those the candle lights are not as those
That animate a mother's reveries ...

This "failure" of course does not mean that Yeats fails "as a poet." His early perception of himself as the poet-priest of "an almost forgotten faith" and his hope that poetry can actually change the world means that his work is *constantly disturbing language, constantly pushing it beyond itself.* If the poem names "swans," we must understand that his language is fundamentally allegorical: it is constantly moving, and to say "swans" is also to say "souls."

In this sense the poet causes (or allows) language to resonate. It is through the particular forms he sees around him that the poet is able to "keep the soul's perception bright and quick to the sounds of above." The language of poetry is fundamentally transformative and leads us to the perception of a larger "world," but the transformation occurs only in the mind of the reader/listener who experiences the poem. It does not change the world, only the particular vessel on which it operates. Poetry does make something happen, but it is only in ourselves that it occurs. Its transformations are not addressed to the world, only to the psyche. The actions of the Irish rebels in "Easter, 1916" create "a terrible beauty," an image of tragic heroism, but, from the point of view of reality, it is quite possible that their death was "needless":

Was it needless death after all?
For England may keep faith
For all that is done and said.
We know their dream; enough
To know they dreamed and are dead;
And what if excess of love
Bewildered them till they died?

Excessive love for what exactly, love *originating* in what exactly? Cf. "Among School Children." What Yeats called "an almost forgotten faith" in

1901 becomes in "The Statues" "that ancient sect," but his attitude in 1938 is very different from his attitude in 1901:

We Irish, born into that ancient sect,
But thrown upon this filthy modern tide,
And by its formless spawning fury wrecked,
Climb to our proper dark, that we may trace
The lineaments of a plummet-measured face.

Not "Buddha's emptiness," only "the statues." *

* One of Yeats' early formulations for the divine state was "Where there is nothing there is God," the title of a 1902 play (later revised as *The Unicorn from the Stars*) and of one of his stories (1896):

'Why is the ruby a symbol of the love of God?'
'Because it is red, like fire, and fire burns up everything, and where there is nothing there is God.'
. . .

At last the abbot said, 'He is none that you have named, for at Easter I had greeting from all, and each was in his brotherhood; but he is Aengus the Lover of God, and the first of those who have gone to live in the wild places and among the wild beasts. Ten years ago he felt the burden of many labours in a brotherhood under the Hill of Patrick and went into the forest that he might labour only with song to the Lord; but the fame of his holiness brought many thousands to his cell, so that a little pride clung to a soul from which all else had been driven. Nine years ago he dressed himself in rags, and from that day none has seen him, unless, indeed, it be true that he has been seen living among the wolves on the mountains and eating the grass of the fields. Let us go to him and bow down before him; for at last, after long seeking, he has found the nothing that is God; and bid him lead us in the pathway he has trodden.

MARVIN COHEN

A Pragmatic Approach

In honor of Marvin Cohen's 91st birthday

**MY POLITICAL PLATFORM
IN A SUPERHUMAN NORM,
YET IN REGULAR ENGLISH FORM.**

What's the best political regime?
"To the top rises the cream?"
No, it's got to be democratic,
unless I'm being erratic.
Let me be simply emphatic.
Every man, woman, and child
must be served, or I'll be riled.
Then you accept my platform?
Make it the everyday norm!
We'll catch the nation by storm!
Will you elect me President
even without a precedent?
Somehow, we'll make a dent
no matter how it's bent!
let's go on it—one hundred percent!
To the public, this my present:
Very Walt Whitmanescue
is my message to the nation.
This be my big bold creation!
Give it your eager elation!
Win it the popular appeal
to co-ordinate all in one congeal!
What a thumping rhythm we all feel!
No, let's quiet it down,
so as not to make all Democrats frown.

**HERE'S ALL THE WHAT'S WHAT
OF ME AND CANDACE WATT,
NEGATING PEOPLE'S NEED TO ASK WHAT.**

Loving Candace Watt
is not a load of rot.
We never had a tot,
being married late,
and slow off the gate.
An ancestry like a Scot
gave her strawberry blond hair.
But that's neither here nor there.
Her soul is big as the globe.
No wonder we had to elobe,
and then were soon to grobe.
Thus all romances evolve,

like plumbers know their valve
of faucets hot or cold.
Knowledge makes us bold
with complete authority,
akin to enlightened morality.
We can dispense with formality
and get on with nitty gritty,
taking excursions into being witty
while keeping up with feeding the kitty.
How privileged, living in the City!
Sophistication is our product
as a real grown-up adult,
thus determining our conduct.
Enjoying life together
occurs independent of weather.
We're not freaky. (We don't wear leather.)
We're frequently apart,
but never threaten to part,
and unlikely ever to start.
Love has deepened
through the years,
and its volume is never in arrears.

**WHAT I WRITE IS LIKE PITCHING.
TO THAT TASK I'M ALWAYS ITCHING,
WITH CLEVER THREADS OF STITCHING.**

As life goes on and on,
what will I base a theme upon
for which to wax poetic?
If nothing, I'm apologetic.
I already used the subject of Death
till I ran out of breath.
I already wrote of sex and women
and gender-based Evolution
for giving babies birth.
I spoke of dimensional earth
and orbiting into outer space.
Can I come up with a new ace
and enter into it face to face?
Sure. I promise readers not to bore them
with trash not worth reading.
To the task can they be worth breeding?
To teach readers how to read,
am I aiming for a new verbal breed?
Then give me a new seed and how to plant.
Sign me up for a new subject to grant.
I'll alert the Muse to inspire me,
and if I'm wild, how to umpire me
to get the ball over the plate.
Perhaps they'll swing too late.
If my fielders behind me do the job,
 I promise the ball not to merely lob,
but spin it like to Ty Cobb.
Should he hit it, let the fielders rob,
with glovework to dazzle,
while I chirp and razzle.

My curve dips and dives
to catch the batters' lives.
When they droop home,
their wives try not to foam.
They go right to sleep
and snore not a peep.
Their dreams forget to move,
since they've lost the groove.

HE'S UP A TREE WHEN IT COMES TO ART. (DIALOGUE)

I've decided to be an artist. Should I be more representational, or more abstract, in my painting?

It depends on which way your talent or genius is branching out.

That sounds too problematical. I want to be sure.

It depends on whether you have a common touch.

Is that a matter of popular appeal?

Let the public decide.

Isn't the public fickle?

Then blame it if you fail.

Good. I have a built-in alibi.

That's the spirit.

But how can I be sure, and take no chances? I don't want to bark up the wrong tree.

Then go out on a limb.

Then I may end up limping, depending on how I land.

It depends on how you branch out.

The multi-colored leaves may block my eyes in the Autumn.

Then you're a Fall guy.

DOMESTIC INFORMATION WITH RHYME OPPORTUNITIES. (DIALOGUE)

Water is good to drink.
It moistens the system and makes you think,
especially during hot weather
and / or if your throat is dry.
So go to the kitchen sink
and turn on the "cold" faucet.
But what if it doesn't work?
Then force it.
So you can be your own plumber.
Also eat food. It makes you plumper.
What if your wife objects?
Then dump her.

OCEANIC DISORDERLINESS

The Specific Ocean featured overlying strata of fish who scorned bottom feeders, being snobbishly obsessed with the status of rank.

The bottom feeders were characteristically devoured down to the bones, including ribs, by the strata immediately on top, who took advantage of their unfair advantage. All this was unknown by human fishermen, who, made courageous by rod-like power, used cheap dead earthworms as unappetizing bait, figuring "What the hell! These fish are too instinctively dumb to know the difference!" Thus, human optimism prevailed, till a whale came along, snobbishly nicknamed "the Prince of Wales," who possessed "the Greediest Appetite of the Sea," in an editorial in "the Fish Bait," an underseas tabloid unreadably wet and chronically crinkled with bits to tear off for scrapbook pasting. It soon went out of print, never having had a leg to stand on, with all the coming and going of riffraft, that made unsightliness the coming mode, according to that new upstart, "The Fish Chronicle," financed by an heir of Neptune. It really made waves, especially at the shore where muscular surfers exploited their handsome human advantage to win the women, who only used fish as a means of appetizing dieting, as editorialized in the "Foam Ranger, cheap for the price. It even puts out a Sand Edition.

A SELF-IMPOSED MEMBER OF THE CLOUD CROWD

A cloud with an inferiority complex was too shy to compete with other (more fluffed out) clouds, for a place in tomorrow's sky pageantry that would feature a parade across the top, followed immediately by a spectacular rain storm just before dark, causing theatregoers inconvenience, who were too fooled by optimistic weather reports to fetch umbrellas.

The inferiority complex was well merited. Its cloud owner was scrawny with grey patchy parts that could barely connect with their major central body.

The other clouds scorned it with contempt. Cloud Land was an Evolution-like struggle for survival and supremacy, like a dog-eat-dog world without the barking.

Anyway, as it turned out, the inferiority-wracked cloud gained enough uncharacter-istic moxie to gate-crash the sky pageantry as its surprising underdog star, indicating there's hope for too-shy competitors in other life competitions unblemished by sentimental endings.

LIFE BEING FUNNY
MAKES IT SADLY SUNNY.

Life is full of wasteful trivia
that mock the sacred objects of our heart.
Although I have the best intent,
let me spend my time in merriment.
Let me afford a laugh or two
to top off inclusion in the human zoo.
So I'll be part of the racket
that puts me in the joyous bracket
of humor's tragic celebration
given to giving up and resignation
of welcoming what's facetious.
It needn't hinder the prestigious,
nor overstress self-conscious pride,
which everyone relents to take in stride.
We're a humble lot, after all,
bruised up and down after our fall.
Having given up on pompous hopes,
serve diminishment to the rank of dopes.
I ride the world in a comet
that swirls and dives but isn't really comic.
Could I help it if it's not authentic?
Pity me. I try to be eccentric.

UNRESOLVED PUZZLE. (DIALOGUE)

Life includes so many things, that I don't know what to make of it. Its complexity bewilders me.
    Why not just live it?
    But that doesn't solve its mystery.
    Just live out its mystery. Ride it.
    But will it penetrate my knowledge?
    Leave it to its own device.
    But I want to understand what life is all about.
    Isn't it just instinctive and intuitive?
    Now you're resorting to mysticism.
    But can't I just invent reality?
    It doesn't work that way. Reality just IS.
    Plain and simple?
    Don't make more of it than what it is.
    But I'm impatient.
    Why bother? Just relax.
    But you have to relax FROM something.
    Then just exert yourself.
    No, that's too arbitrary.
    Are you trying to create meaning?
    It just turns out that way.
    Well, build on it.
    What is "it"?
    You're too reductive.

FLOWERS AND BIRDS
ARE JUST BEYOND WORDS.

The flowers that bloom in the Spring,
unlike the birds that are on the wing,
are exclusively rooted to the ground,
whereby the birds can fly around.
So flowers, immobile, have insufficient
    exercise.
On the other hand, every bird flies
to exercise feathery muscles,
unlike the flower, who tussles
with being stuck to the ground,
with innate difficulty to get around,
being by nature eternally earth-bound.
Need I explain this any further?
I'm sure you get my point
of how things operate in this joint.

HOW LOVE GETS SO OUT OF HAND,
IT CAN HARDLY BE CONSIDERED BLAND.
OUR CLOSE FEELINGS BECOME FIRST-HAND.

Love is back-and-forth fellow feelings,
at low ebbs sometimes, but then ceilings,
too obvious to be concealing.
Each to the other asks, "How are you feeling?"
The answer is: "Since you're mine,
I rate your status as divine.
Your body is so well proportioned
that I have to be extra cautioned
not to hug you too tight
in a demonstration of my ferocious might.
I may break your ribs by squeezing too tight,
causing you to be reduced to a cripple.
My apologies multiply to triple.
Then into some wine bottles I must tipple.
You imbibe too, till we're both so high
as to take twin transports into the sky,
to join the birds wherein they fly.
Close to heaven, therein we cry."

WARNINGS AND SCARE
GIVE YOU A NIGHTMARE,
SO INTO THE VACANCY YOU STARE.

To be able to avert a fearful disaster,
and run away from it faster,
put yourself under the protection of Fear,
so imminent danger won't get too near.
Then cling to the consolations of safety,
and enjoy the comforts of coffee and pastry.
To get away QUICKER from disaster,
PANIC will enable you to run even faster.
Again, take refuge under sweet Fear,

that prevents a horrible outcome from
     coming too near.
Always look behind you to guard the arrear,
so you won't give yourself too bum a steer.
All glory to your protector: Fear,
without which, you would have been long dead,
with many atrocities damaging your head,
so you even take too much refuge in your bed
to escape, via sleep and dreams,
from nightmarish screams.
All is not quite the same way it seems.

FEAR OF WATER
PREVENTS A LIQUID SLAUGHTER.
AVOID SEA-DEATH
BY KEEPING DRY YOUR BREATH.

(1)
Before risking a boat ride, I take a peek
at the bottom, to see if there's a leak.
This is precaution against drowning.
Who wants to be crowning
his own demise at the sea's bottom,
all because down below was rotten?
When the brine gets into my lungs,
I'm so scared that I release my dungs.
Reader, let this not happen to you.
The bottom contains too fishy a view
if you read that leak all the way through.

(2)
So cling to your safety above all,
so out of the mud you won't have to crawl.
When you're about to enter a boat,
be certain it will be able to float.
Once assured, be happy and gloat.
Then away you'll go sailing,
every precaution now availing
to prevent any future ailing.
Don't be victim to a watery splash
that eventually consigns your corpse to ash.

WHAT DID ROBERT BURNS MEAN?
(DIALOGUE)

In his famous New Year's Eve song, the
Scottish poet Robert Burns advocated we all
"raise a cup of comfort" to old acquaintances.
But he neglected to mention what that cup of
comfort should contain.
    Presumably, alcohol.
    I've already assumed that. But should it be
cheap wine or expensive champagne?
    Maybe just beer.
    Imported foreign beer? Or domestic?
    He left it to the host's bank account, or to what
was available in the given bar or tavern. He
didn't need to specify, like a pedantic pedant.
He was not a scientist, only a poet. Mainly, he
wanted to capture the spirit of the occasion.
    Which was what?
    That we should REMEMBER old
acquaintances.
    But he neglected to say which ones.
    The poem was too short to include a whole
list. He must have assumed that everyone
present had his own individual list.
    I think he left too much to chance.
    He must have been drunk when he wrote that
poem. After all, he was only a Scot.
    But not all Scots were poets.
    Good. They had to get on with practical things
in order to have an honorable relation with
their southern neighbor, England.
    But England was more famous.
    No wonder. They invented our language.
    But the Scots copied it.
    That's legal. They had open borders.

A DAISY, LIKE OTHER KINDS OF FLOWER,
DWELLS BRIEFLY IN THE SPRINGTIME
HOUR. (PART DIALOGUE)

How are you feeling?

Like blah. Lackadaisical.

Then if you lack a daisy, redeem it by picking or
buying a lilac, iris, tulip, any other flower
dwelling in our holy Springtime hour.

But isn't this nomenclature
of names coming from nature?

Such as creepy insects and vermin?

Stop your loathsome sermon!

I'm busy, must hurry, see you later,
when our leisure time is greater,
like a nutty poem creator
whose head dwells in a cloud.
His poems made him proud
whenever society allowed
him to recite them out loud,
even to a hostile, mocking crowd.
He picked a daisy and stuck it in his lapel,
where for two vacant days that daisy would dwell.
On his audience he remembered casting a spell.

THE BIOGRAPHER'S SUBJECT.

(1)
If you're caught in the coils of death,
and consequently are devoid of breath,

you're passive and crumble to dust.
You can't get back to life again,
and have no friend to help you.
Your predicament is so impossible
that emptiness has you trapped.
Yet in your life, you were often rapt
with mentality, passion, and love.
NOW in your grave, THEN you were above.
What a difference time makes!
Now you're on its death side,
where you contradictorily "reside."
I describe you in your helpless state.
Remotely, that's how we relate.
Did I ever know you once before?
No, but as your biographer I aim for your core.

(2)
The describer and the described.
Each is a stranger to the other's "vibe."
But the biographer, to do his job,
has to capture his subject's throb.

ABOUT JAZZ.
(dedicated to Judge Peter Jackson.)

In New Orleans, where they invented jazz,
the new sound was allowed to pass
the censorship, and be decidedly up-beat,
so for normal kinds of music it sounded defeat.
Jazz became hot all around the world,
so into the arms of respectability it was twirled.
Anybody guilty of hearing a different sound
was forced to hear jazz with his arms bound.
That's where jazz won its foremost aspect,
to win everybody's (without exception) respect.
So now that jazz is at the top of the musical tables,
its noble practitioners are the heroes of exaggerated
      fables.
Jazz is so known for its captivating rhythm,
which prominently wins the sheer delight of her
      or him.
It's based not only on deliberation, but on whim.
Conventional musicians have gone to ground, grim.
They've abandoned music and taken a
      permanent swim.

WHY CRITICS ARE ABSOLUTELY
NECESSARY
TO PREVENT IMPERFECTION FROM
ROAMING MERRY.

When your musical creation has a sour note,
"Delete it!" is the prevailing critical vote.
Any work of art that's quite imperfect
should give a ruthless goodbye to its prominent
      defect.

A painting should have such impeccable unity,
that a false color should leave without impunity.
A sculpture whose sculptor added a sixth finger
should not allow that marble or granite to linger.
Any poem written for the heart
should eagerly see a disharmonious rhyme depart.
Such is the unsparing nature of every art.
Therefore, a novel whose heroine is immoral
should not have its second edition under restoral.

PARDON MY SUBJECT: DEATH.

The nightmare of Death is all too real.
But once it happens, you can't feel.
Nevertheless, anaesthesia
can't help making Death easier.
It makes you so numb
that mentally you feel quite dumb.
As for the matter of pain,
it's too absent for you to complain.
To do so, then, is against the grain.
Consciousness is so oblivious
that it need not be taken serious.
You can get away with not being there,
allowing other people to impolitely stare
at nothing at all, but you USED to be there.
After all, people should make an effort to care.
Anyway, Death is used to being ignored,
So to keep up appearances, don't act bored.
Ask Death, "How was your former life?"
His answer might well be: "Not bad, but too
      much strife.
Death seems only second-rate,
but I won't insult it, such being my fate."

A PRAGMATIC APPROACH.
(ASSUMING I'M YOUR COACH.)

Rectify what's wrong
by making a change.
But if things are already OK,
keep them going the same way.
Play the radical
when things are radically wrong.
Play the conservative
when you've struck the right way to live.
Live of course in your comfort zone
where things come into their own.
But depression and melancholy
need a new tack to make things jolly.
In that case, not to change is folly.
So see what's going on
for what to base your strategy upon.
Judge what's the product
of your recent conduct.
Preserve it or revise

according to what seems wise.
Then you'll be a wise guy,
according to the way the wind will fly.
The future can be engineered
depending on what you enjoyed or feared,
but don't be deceived by what only appeared.
To whatever goes on, be geared.
On the eve itself, be happy new yeared,
so with plenty to drink, be cheered.
But if you don't play up, be jeered.

A LIFETIME OF MEMORIES.

Life keeps going on, but when will it stop?
Not until you're ready to drop.
When you're at the end of your rope,
the time has come to perhaps give up.
A good time was had by all, but the party's over.
Stop in your tracks. You're no longer a rover.
Throw the empty bottles in the garbage
even though they crack and break,
which does the environment no good.
Show your loyalty to the neighborhood.
Clean up with might and main.
To be a sloppy neighbor? Refrain.
Dump your belongings in the alley?
Keep peace between the mountain and the valley.
All this is your roaming territory.
Don't let this tale be a terror story.
Embrace your neighbor, since life succumbs to
     death,
and wish your lungs goodbye, with all their
     precious breath.
Pump yourself full of air.
Now you've officially become your father's heir.
You've graduated from adolescence,
and joined the world in coalescence.

YOUR SERVANT-LIKE PARENTS
ARE ALWAYS AVAILABLE, IT'S APPARENT.
THEY HUMBLY TRY TO BE TRANSPARENT.
DO THEY CRITICIZE YOU? THEY DAREN'T.

When you're born, you're waited on by available
     parents,
who serve you at your mercy
like rich people's servants.
They ought to wear livery.
They were there at your delivery.
They take on such full responsibility
to the best of their joint ability,
as a convenient suitability.
Of course, they pay the bill.
They do your every will,
with painstaking obedience
at your constant expedience,

at your immedient frequence.
Are you thankful and grateful?
Not enough so.
THEY should thank YOU
for such a glorious privilege?
That's how spoiled YOU are,
and embroiled THEY are.
They deserve a medallion star.
In reality, you're a little brat.
Past adolescence, you engage them in a spat,
and obscenely call them a pair of outworn rats
ridiculously afraid of any harmless cats.
Thus you mock them without mercy
in your rented flat in New Jersey.
They, of course, pay the rent,
even though they're old and bent,
and their pride has been long spent.
What a monster I'll grow up to be!
Reader, don't endeavor to be like me.
Between me and morality, we don't agree.

HOW THE POOR OLD MAN COMES OUT
AHEAD,
HAVING SAVED MONEY JUST BY BEING DEAD.
HOWEVER, ALL THAT DRINK HE HAD
WENT TO HIS HEAD.

Life is too valuable to lose.
But Death says: "You can't choose."
So what can you do? Try booze.
Knowing you're going to lose,
drink gin, beer, and whisky,
making you so vitally frisky.
To be sure, drink extra wine.
So when Death comes, you won't whine.
With all that booze, you won't need to dine.
So then you're sure to come out a winner,
by saving money (not paying for dinner).
But by not paying for the drinks,
the bartender is angry while your life sinks.
He calls you "a cheapstake who morally stinks."

DICHOTOMY DUOS

male/female man/woman life/death old/young
left/right good/bad day/night light/dark
straight/crooked natural/artificial strong/weak
happy/sad new/old healthy/sick round/flat
in/out heavy/light long/short high/low right/left
right/wrong intelligent/stupid rough/smooth wet/dry
soft/hard long/short thick/thin fat/skinny win/lose
fast/slow solid/liquid gay/straight early/late
many/few easy/hard drunk/sober full/empty
yes/no far/near genuine/phony real/fake true/false

BASEBALL DICHOTOMY DUOS

ball/strike fair/foul safe/out win/lose

SUGARCOATING DEATH
WITH A SWEETENING ELIXIR
FOR A ROMANTIC FIXTURE.

You sink into the amorous arms of Death,
who kisses away your final breath,
and conveys you to eternity's honeymoon.
How orderly for you to swoon!
Death loves your easy submission
to his otherwise morbid commission.
In this romantic atmosphere,
don't spoil it by introducing the note of fear.
You and divine Death must call each other "dear."
You're his eternally sexy bride,
so agree sweetly to his taking you for a ride.
Death is such a seductive sweetheart
that he's only doing, per script, his part.
Now it's time for you to faint away
and allow night to steal your previous day.

THE PROFESSION OF WRITING
CAN BE SO EXCITING
THAT ALL THE FISH ARE BITING.

Being a writer
is a great self-exciter.
It provokes such enthusiasm
as to promote almost an orgasm.
But being a writer should demand a public.
So hire a good press agent
to install your glorious pageant.
If you don't succeed, be patient.
Success is sure to come.
The public can't be that dumb
as to overlook your quality
in writing such successful verse
that you don't even have to rehearse.
It came out beautiful in its first draft.
To prove it, I'll give you a carbon copy of the graph.
It's comical, so you'll have a good laugh.
Since all my fans want my autograph,
I had to hire a complete press office staff
to cover my wholesale success.
I must beware, though, of immoderate excess.
They say that moderation will overtake regret,
so don't risk your winnings with a losing bet.
Stack up your well-earned gains,
and see if a substantial amount remains
to coarsely waste on the horses and dames.
Each will provoke the according shames.

THE ELEMENT OF SURPRISE
CAN'T BE ANTICIPATED,
WHICH WOULD MAKE IT DISSIPATED.

Can you expect to be surprised
by the night being eclipsed by the sunrise?
No. A surprise has to be spontaneous.
By expecting it, you spoil its wizardry
by taking away its mystery.
Put your expectations under wrap
by not making them prematurely rapt,
as you, a spoilsport, are apt.
Allow your surprise to pleasantly unfold
when you suddenly see this lump of lead is gold.
Your surprise thus had an element of being bold.
Enjoy lots of such cases, before being too old.

WHY ME AND NOT YOU?
LET'S LOOK IT UP IN "WHO'S WHO?"
AND SEIZE UPON THE HIDDEN CLUE.

How did I turn out to be me,
gravitating to that particular identity,
instead of my genes choosing you
as a role model to pursue?
Evolution's cunning engineering
haphazardly swayed my direction
to take on my parents' infection,
giving me the ingredients
to fit the mold of expedience
as perpendicular to my eventual outcome.
So I became a stockholder instead of a bum.
Give me the answer to this: How come?
Well, it's all a mysterious process,
slanted to the eventual end
as the railroad suddenly switched tracks
and ended to confront my own backs.
This swayed the way I became,
given the label chosen for my name.
Helpless, I turned out to be me,
a seeming destination I couldn't flee.

WHAT I ADVOCATE
IS THE WORLD IN A BENIGN STATE.

(1)
Here's what I root for,
being against brute force
as humanity's inevitable course.
Don't you also endorse
kindness and goodness to take over
as the over-all man and woman lover?
May the wings of peace hover.

(2)

I'm the caretaker of the human zoo.
I carefully notate who's who.
I'm Evolution's current representative,
whose policy is preventative.
I resist the spread of anarchy
that makes me weep into my hankies
if the World Series winner isn't the Yankees.
I advocate kindness for human kind
to prevent morality from going blind.
I want justice and compassion
to be the universal passion,
which is currently not the fashion.
let's prevent all wars.
Death and suffering are not adored.
May mercy and goodness be fated
over that awful rat—hatred.
Every human is sacred.
Donate your love for the human race
to operate at a successful pace
and come out winning, on top.
Good luck to our human crop.

I WAS TOO AMBITIOUS
FOR MY DINNERS TO REMAIN DELICIOUS.

Living forever is my great ideal,
but mortality offers no such deal.
I've got to reduce my desire.
It's too high that I aspire.
I'll only live a more modest sum,
and not the total that strikes everyone dumb
as too brash and greedy.
I'm accused of being too needy.
I'll slow down into extreme old age,
and barely exist beyond that tottering page.
I'll crumble into a heap of dust,
as every ancient veteran of life must.
So tearfully wish me goodbye now,
bearing deep doom as the sure sign on my brow.
Along with my body, my memories will go,
and disappear into the universal flow,
as though their happenings never occurred.
I turn rigid as though not once having stirred.
I exist like an architectural monument
that travels nowhere, with no momentum.
For my taste, it's too humdrum
to hear the silent monotony,
instead of capitalistically grasping monopoly.

MY POETIC PROFITS
WERE PREDICTED BY FINANCIAL
PROPHETS.

My poem takes a whimsical turn,
with plenty of space left to burn.
Will the carefully wrought lines coalesce?

They will, I hope, more or less.
Let not the empty space be left blank.
Complete your poem's meaning if you want the
    reader to thank
you for plowing through,
with still more later lines left to do.
Oh what a laborious business is writing poetry!
The financial economy is dependent
on the inspired poet being independent,
with profit on the bottom line
to carefully design
and reasonably align.
Can translated poems visit another country?
Sure. We all want foreign readers to be comfy.
After using so many reams of paper,
you would expect my usual eloquence to taper.
All the trees that are chopped down
turn into paper to illuminate my crown.
If I have an inspiration, I don't let it hang,
but submit it to readership with a bang.
Publishers are delirious with delight
when their prospects prosper due to my poetic might.
They fill my coffers with so many dollars
that all my press agents contribute their hollers.
Writing poetry has so enhanced my life
that its money I earned bought me a beautiful wife
whom I hire to be my Muse
over whom all my readers enthuse.
With this success, I know only bliss,
highlighted by my wife's resounding kiss.

CORRECTING A MISTAKE.
(MY ORIGINAL ASSUMPTION WAS FAKE.)

Nostalgia is both sweet and sour,
like a delicious Chinese dish
you ate instead of fish.
Some of your memories are blotted out
by mere forgetfulness over the years.
Your brain was the culprit,
like the aviator in the cockpit
caused the plane to crash,
causing innocent lives to smash.
But what was my topic? I forgot.
I was momentarily up in the air,
but didn't treat the pilot fair.
It wasn't his fault the plane crashed.
It was an engineering cause,
a mechanical defect
in the plane itself.
So to the pilot I apologize,
and now bring my accuracy up to size.
I'm glad I realistically corrected my mistake
before the reader would do a double-take.
It's about time I would wake.
Hello, reader, now I've revived.
Meanwhile, has your patience survived?

TO A HEAVEN SEEKER
WHOSE REMOTE POSSIBILITY CAN'T BE
BLEAKER.

Being dead is impossible to recover from,
so the very attempt identifies you as dumb.
Give up your determination for life's renewal.
What organic matter can you use as fuel?
Whoever ridicules you, challenge him to a duel,
with the loser having the right to be called a fool.
Idiotic stupidity rules the underworld,
where the acute brains of intellect are never unfurled.
Being dead is an inescapable trap,
in the form of a package you can never unwrap,
whose ribbons are permanently knotted,
which is the way Death originally had it plotted.
Therefore heaven is out of your reach,
like feeding a dead whale on a sandy beach.

THE POEM UNDER CONSTRUCTION
WILL FERRET OUT ITS OWN REDUCTION,
SELF-ELIMINATING LIKE A SUCTION.

As a poem goes speeding along
like a rhythmic song,
find words precisely
to fit the united theme,
tributaries to a stream.
Consider the whole deal as a pack
magnetized to what to attack.
Then stack the whole deck
and rescue it out of its wreck.
All the words should be one of a piece,
and aspire to one unified release.
The whole, made up of allied parts,
should start itself to its right ends,
and end exactly on a dot
that contains the weight of the whole lot.
Then, once the poem is complete,
consider it as a finished feat.
Stop there at the final line
to which the preceding will align.
Has it found its own design?
Yes, and thank god it's mine.

THE CLOUD AND THE CLOCK
HAD A FIGHT. DID THEY ROCK!

A cloud and a clock had a competition.
If it came to a draw, there'd be a repetition.
The cloud claimed the advantage of height.
The clock claimed a mechanical superiority
by mechanistic expertese.
The cloud claimed it could float on a breeze.
The clock claimed to be so timely

that the cloud diminished to tiny.
Juries and referees came in to judge,
but neither side was willing to budge.
A math expert came in, knowing high division.
Each side regarded the other with derision.
So when a verdict was given, it was "no decision."
But the cloud and the clock figured it out
that the result would remain in permanent doubt.
Thus harmony won out between the opponents,
leading each to hug its individual components.

HOW TO LIVE BETTER,
PRECISELY TO THE LETTER,
AS A FAULTY GO-GETTER.

(1)
When I was an embryo in my mother's womb,
little did I realize I'd find a tomb
at the other end of my life's span—
completely improvised without a plan.
Sunshine interrupted produces a shadow
which doesn't make a dent—it's too shallow.
The inconvenience of life
shows much evidence of its strife.

(2)
When life succeeds in getting you down,
try to pretend that you're wearing a royal crown,
and can lord it over all the citizenry,
and even mow them down, like artillery.
If you're too thirsty, go to a distillery
and avail yourself of the sample drink
so intoxicating, you can't think.
You even get free food in the bargain,
affording an opportunity to hog again,
and protrude your stomach so obese
that your belt unbuckles with a loud release.
But it doesn't give you any extra ounce of ease,
once you pull out from your ungainly squeeze.
Life, in fact, is a tough fit.
Find many more things that you can omit.
Thus a shrunken universe
can be played well in reverse,
provided with due diligence you rehearse.
The world isn't yet ready for your hearse.
Find your crowd, and with them disperse.
Then, isolated from the group,
re-organize, and march with your troop.

THE BAR.

When it was my turn to pay for our democratic
   round of drink,
my presence would somehow mysteriously
   shrink.

My parasitical reputation would ignominiously
    stink.
When it was my turn, as the wheel spun, to pay,
there would confoundedly come up an
    unaccountable delay.
But I turned out to suffer financial
    embarrassment,
which subjected me to a round of physical
    harassment
by my unruly so-called mates.
How mystifying it was that I should mysteriously
    delay
in slow degrees to take out my wallet and pay!
This was noticeable to the whole bar,
which caused me from then on to be barred
ever from entering these premises again.
When would the ban be lifted?
When my financial fortunes had shifted.
Ah, would I ever be so gifted?
Thus my throat grew increasingly dry,
lacking for a remedial alcoholic supply,
and I wondered: "Is it now my turn to die?"
But the bar took up a philanthropic collection
to rescue me momentarily from monetary
    misfortune.
It was barely enough, but not quite a fortune.
From then on, I was openly admitted
whenever my arrival I humbly submitted.
I had to leave my pride at home
when into this fatal bar I'd roam.

THE VULGARITY OF HOW TO EAT
MAKES DELICATE ELEGANCE RETREAT,
AND DRIVES ME TO THE TOILET FOR A SEAT.

Whenever I go into the kitchen,
the appetite on my belly starts itchin',
so if I don't get food, I'll start bitchin'.
I fill my belly to an obese extent,
so I don't know where my slim figure went,
since all my extra poundage has been spent
on excess pleasure at the table.
To fill my belly, I'm more than able.
Then, puffed up like a frog or toad,
I have to go to discharge my load
into the bathroom's ivory toilet.
If that's too difficult? I'll toil it.
If it won't come out of my ass? I'll oil it.
Any remains of left-over food? I'll boil it.
Why waste any food at all?
Get the left-over at the toilet stall.
If you mix up digestion and elimination,
remember that you're a patriot of this fine nation.

A SO-CALLED FUTURE.

Throughout my life, I've always had some kind
    of future.
But now, at ninety plus, I barely have any.
So I proceed to invent imaginary ones
that serve as unreachable daydreams
describing a whole lot of impractical schemes.
All the stationery I waste in reams
to write down these elaborate devices
can be crumbled up. And my future's gone,
like a dead old swan on a dirty pond
I spend remaining life to ponder upon.
Why not my own human past,
whose effect on me was so vast?
I too much mourn that it couldn't last.
Before that, it was one big beautiful blast.
My bony hand crumbles my baldness
into bundles of imaginary hair
that realistically just aren't there.
My brainless skull conceives of cloudless air
in an empty universe where corpses stare.
Am I then about to croak?
I'm sorry. This is no joke.
So now that I'm about to relinquish my state,
with whom can I conduct an endless debate?
Myself, if I can find him,
so continually assigned him.
Together, we'll be both dim.

THE WRITER'S CAREER
FLIRTED WITH FEAR,
THEN REGAINED ITS HOPEFUL CHEER.

Pursuing inspiration as a writer,
I got bogged down. So then I became a fighter
in the game of fooling around with the written word.
But my efforts turned out absurd.
Readers tried in vain to make sense,
but the lines I wrote got nowhere—too dense.
They gave no readers a lift
from my so-called literary gift.
My method of writing was to emphasize thrift,
by saying the most in the fewest words.
But I filled my stationery with waste,
and had to resort to glue or paste.
Maybe I simply lacked taste?
I appealed to publishers in vain.
To reject me, those scum couldn't refrain.
So what happened to my profession?
It flew away from my possession,
leading to an almost clinical depression.
But then I made a comeback,
and leapfrogged to fame on celebrity's back.
To redeem myself, how had I taken the right track?
That remains a total mystery,
unable to trace my creative history

in the strange and weird inner world
from which arbitrary words became unfurled.

GOING OPPOSITE THE WELCOME MAT,
UNDIGNIFIED, TO BE SPIT AT.
DISHONORED INTO THE GRAVE,
WHETHER WE WERE COWARDLY OR BRAVE.

When life fades to its declining years,
we're bundled up and put away
in nursing homes to be cared for
like babies helpless recently born.
We're torn away from independence
and organized into units.
We're guided like sheep or infants.
Old age. We're hopelessly led to die
with rebelling memories that wish to stay
in independent self-sufficient array.
But memories are impotent to reclaim that day.
So we sink down into our hellhole graves,
dim of our former consciousness.
We're treated like inanimate objects,
totally powerless to object.
We take up ultra-valuable space,
and placed in the category of "erase,"
without the benefit of dignity or grace.

HOW I LOWERED MY FAMILY'S REPUTATION
WHO HAVE ME AS A SON, PUT ON PROBATION.

I'm too poor, and have got to steal,
being too hungry to afford a meal.
I hope none of my friends will squeal
to detectives that I'm a crook,
so they'll just have to book
me as a full-fledged thief
whose crimes dip below belief.
How my parents would be brought to grief!
They'll pretend they're only my uncle and aunt,
to soften the family blow
that threatens to drop our reputation below
the official big dignity mark.
They'll cap it off with a vulgar remark
barely whispered in the brazen dark,
where the dogs woof amiss at the trees' bark,
and some poor beggars go around stark.
Oh, let me restore my family's good name,
currently ranked with those below shame,
whose aspirations missed the mark, being lame
enough to shock any guy or dame
who went through life without an aim.
They were known to collectively fail.

No wonder. They were beyond the pale.
In advertising, they inspired "no sale!",
so were easily fired from their job,
like not catching a ball tossed in a lob.
They acted the role of a poor slob.
Back home, their sad wives would sob
in misery and plan divorce
to revenge the family who ran off course.
This is merely some families' tragic loss
by failing to please the imperious boss.

HERE'S MY REMAINING FATE.
IT'S NOT QUITE FIRST-RATE.

What's next on my agenda,
having to be life's spender,
with no more prospect of splendor
except the option to surrender?
I've squandered my entire youth,
leaving old age to be my final truth.
Can I protest? No, I'm mute.
After all this, then what's left?
The dubious privilege of being bereft.
Wonderful times happened to me.
But now my rusty ghost yearns to be free.
Medically I've so deteriorated
that my chances of survival are nil-rated.
To doom and Death I'm fated.
Will future hope make me elated?
No. Things are even worse than stated.
If I'm still pleading for the element of hope,
I should give up, unless I'm a prize dope,
having reached already the end of my rope.
With blind eyes, where can I further grope?
Happening to meet Death by chance,
I kiss goodbye to Life's romance,
and tear up my Invitation to the Dance.

PAUL KAVANAGH

CHAMBER

The characters within are all inventions and bear no resemblance to living persons. Only the writer is real.

Martha Smith-Winstanley arrives predictably late apologetic Russian literature apologetic red in the face blowing (Joyce's *Ulysses* couldn't help myself) and sits afore removing her raindrenched coat and silk scarf. Afore Martha Smith-Winstanley sits Henry Montegut and betwixt is the table not incongruous of a restaurant in London Paris New York with ornate decorations and three candles aflame. "Martha my dear," says Henry. Martha Smith-Winstanley titters afore apologizing once again and then ignores Henry to survey the byzantine room. "This is serpentine," says Martha. This is her first occasion her first occasion within but not without. The sustenance is splendid she has been told from without and without she inhales and agrees. Henry Montegut already with wine pours two glasses but a grimace betrays. Finally, Martha Smith-Winstanley divests the raindrenched coat and silk scarf. Wait. Let's continue. "Yes," admits Henry, "I've already indulged." An obsequious waiter takes away the raindrenched coat and silk scarf. "The lips betrayed you," says Martha. Henry Montegut swills. Martha aims for the light. Henry smells. Martha Smith-Winstanley empties the glass in one movement and sighs as she recognizes the chamber music. Henry Montegut tuts loudly also recognizing the chamber music. Martha Smith-Winstanley offers her glass and hums flagrantly. Henry Montegut pours and spills wine. Numerous tables in the environs are disturbed. A patron complains to an obsequious waiter. Another patron complains. Martha Smith-Winstanley pleads for support but is still defiant. Henry Montegut pours and spills more wine. The Doyenne approaches the table and politely but firmly asks for equanimity. Martha Smith-Winstanley guffaws manifesting her joy at the disequilibrium spreading. Henry Montegut points and says, "Ophelia no Desdemona must perform." The Doyenne pleads for composure. Martha Smith-Winstanley drinks the wine laughing wine spilling a breast slipping and sliding the wine cascading down her chin upon the now exposed breast. A protrude of little to no merit. Henry Montegut swears. The Doyenne demands decorum. Patrons coalesce. Martha Smith-Winstanley shatters a glass. The Doyenne points to the double doors and with fingers folding and straightening articulates action. The double doors open. Four waiters push forward the Bull of Phalaris. Disturbed and perturbed the Patrons stand and briskly and excitedly (Romans at the Colosseum) congregate at the undisciplined table. There we witness drooling dribbling spitting erect nipples flushed skin sweat beads the size of hardons galore. The Doyenne gives the command. The Patrons stand Martha Smith-Winstanley and Henry Montegut and remove the clothing of Martha Smith-Winstanley and Henry Montegut. A waiter strikes a match off the sole of a boot (A match is a tool for starting a fire. Typically, matches are made of small wooden sticks or stiff paper. One end is coated with a material that can be ignited by friction generated by striking the match against a suitable surface.) and lights the fire under the Bull of Phalaris. Through the bronze opened door Martha Smith-Winstanley and Henry Montegut are jostled into the hollow belly of the Bull. The door is locked from the outside. Flames rage. Through the nostrils of the Bull Martha Smith-Winstanley and Henry Montegut screams are metamorphosed into the grunt of a Bull sexed. Out of the ascending smoke of spicy clouds of incense appears Emily Darling. A petite girl with a proclivity for floral dresses and staid shoes. Under her arm without ostentatiousness but inevitably ostentatious you will see Milton's *Paradise Lost*. Emily Darling is waiting for the train to take her home. Emily Darling has spent a delightful day in the city. The train approaches. Emily Darling sighs remorsefully. Soon the city will be a dream an ignis fatuous. The book slips. Emily Darling stoops. The train slows. Emily Darling trips and like Anna Karenina is cut in two by the train's myriad impassive steel wheels. Out of the blood and the guts and the weeping of pure sorrow at the loss of an innocent sighs Alan Boorman. He stands afore us bored of life of sex of death. Alan Boorman is nondescript and happily overjoyed to be nondescript and fashionably bored. "To be is to—" I stop Alan Boorman midsentence. Enough I say. With the wave of a hand I conjure Malacoda Scarmiglione Alichino Calcabrina Cagnazzo Libicocco Draghignazzo Ciriatto Graffiacane Farfarello Rubicante and the unnamed one and at my bidding they (awful beasts that they are) drag Alan Boorman screaming and pissing and shitting and vomiting down to Malebolge. John Jacobs was never happy. Already I am sick of John Jacobs. The name makes me want to puke. I hate the name thus the man. Blistering boils and putrid pus I cover his body with from head to toe from arse to tit. What a body thin and frail creaking and groaning. He pisses yellow flux and shits worms. I hate the body the more I see of it with its plights and gripes it pollutes the mind. Cabbages under the armpits and sores hemorrhaging running up and down the legs and arms. Death will not appear for another hundred years I guess a biblical death I surmise. Alice Little stands before me naked as the day she was born I cherish her breasts firm and nipples erect and desire her pudenda lightly trimmed and lips magnetic to my lips I am helpless I must gravitate I want her I want her she must be mine and mine alone her hair is a cascade of fire and her eyes emerald green the cliches worry me not her skin white as alabaster and not a hint of superfluous fat (well some on her lovely derriere and her nape Oh I love a fat nape) she is no Botticellian babe mustered out of scum with incongruously large hands and elongated chubby belly no but wait here is Alice Little and Alice Little will not succumb to my charms for she is Aristocracy and I am a Pauper. So, for a thousand years Alice Little will stand before me and I will fashion her to my will and whims and I will open the pit the stage the gallery (think Elizabethan shitholes) and Alice Little will be molested by me and only me and the pox the syphilis will spread and the thieves the soldiers the mercenaries will fight a myriad of Iagos and drink and copulate and expectorate and micturate and defecate and the alchemists will cast spells and Alice Little will sigh a Shakespearean sigh may be too Shakespearean may be more than a hint Sophoclean yes Sophoclean it has to be Sophoclean (I hate myself with all this Greek Stuff) "Why was I birthed" she will cry I will cry and I have no answer except may be vanity yes vanity and this torture chamber should be designed and built by Giovanni Battista Piranesi and housed by Miguel de Cervantes Saavedra and Count Lev Nikolayevich Tolstoy and made into a movie by Peter Greenaway for that is what I deserve for this chamber I have fashioned.

KURT LUCHS

SWEARING ON HIS LIFE: ETHERIDGE KNIGHT IN THE PRISON OF LONELINESS

The poet and critic Malcom Cowley once referred to the writer Conrad Aiken as "the buried giant of American literature," a fair assessment to anyone familiar with Aiken's poetry, novels, short stories and autobiography. In a similar fashion, Etheridge Knight could be called the buried giant of the Black Arts Movement of the sixties and seventies. His work was recognized and celebrated during his lifetime, to be sure. And he is remembered today, with several of his poems attaining the stature of American classics, such as the much-anthologized "The Idea of Ancestry" "The Bones of My Father," and the one we'll be looking at here, "Feeling Fucked Up." Yet he is nowhere near as famous as other BAM luminaries, such as Maya Angelou and Nikki Giovanni and the founder of the movement, Amiri Baraka (aka Leroi Jones).

There are several reasons, none of them having anything to do with the quality of his work. He didn't start writing until he was in his thirties while serving a sentence for armed robbery. Before that he grew up in poverty in Mississippi and Kentucky, one of seven children. Despite reportedly being a brilliant student he dropped out of school in the eighth grade and immediately went to work. In 1947 he joined the Army where he served 10 years, seeing battle in Korea and receiving a shrapnel wound that left him with chronic pain and a morphine habit that he would struggle with for most of life. Engaging in robbery to feed his habit led him to prison. And there, after his initial rage cooled, he began to turn his life around. He studied. He read voraciously. He found an outlet in poetry and determined to become a great writer.

By the time of his release in 1968 he had achieved that goal, publishing his first book, *Poems from Prison*, which was widely praised inside and outside the Black literary community (Gwendolyn Brooks and Donald Hall were both fans, among many others). There followed more than two decades of writing and four further books before he died of lung cancer in 1991 at the age of 59. He had overcome much and accomplished much. But he started late and died relatively young, and that no doubt affected his reputation in the long run. His work is still not nearly as well-known as it should be. Another factor here is that more than three decades after his death Etheridge Knight has yet to see a *Collected Poems*. A selected volume called *The Essential Etheridge Knight* from 1986 comes the closest, although it is far from complete and contains nothing from his last five years. To borrow a phrase from the poem of his we're looking at today, that is fucked up. Somebody should do something about it.

"Feeling Fucked Up" is atypical of Knight in that he doesn't normally employ profanity. In this poem he drops a total of 14 f-bombs, including the one in the title and the "mothafucking" near the end. Profanity is a strong spice, to be used sparingly most of the time. However, there are occasions when unleashing a stream of curses makes perfect sense. When you accidentally hit your thumb with a hammer. When another driver cuts you off in traffic. When your bare foot steps on something squishy and wet, and you realize your cat failed to make it to the box again. And when your lover leaves you.

It is this last circumstance, one familiar to nearly everybody, that Knight addresses in this poem. The poem is in free verse consisting of two stanzas, the first being seven lines long and the second being 11 lines. Aside from the title, all of the swearing occurs in the second stanza.

The first line of the poem establishes both the situation and the author's colloquial tone, drawing from the idiom of the blues: "Lord she's gone done left me done packed / up and split." That forward slash within the line is a technique Knight uses frequently. It can be read different ways depending on the context—perhaps an ad-

46

ditional break within the line, or setting apart a certain phrase. Here I take it to imply two readings with one phrase: she packed up and split in one continuous motion, one memory; and also she packed up and then split, two separate actions, drawn out as they happen. The latter reading sounds as if the author watched her do both of these things, leading to the buildup of grief, pain and anger that fuels the second stanza.

The rest of stanza one immediately dives into sharp feelings of loss:

> . . . everywhere the world is bare
> bright bone white   crystal sand glistens

The extra spaces between "white" and "crystal" effectively underscore the emptiness of a beach scene that is still beautiful but lacking the only beauty that matters now, the one that is no longer there. Stanza one concludes with an increasingly anguished cry of despair that perfectly sets up the outburst that will follow in stanza two:

> dope death dead dying and jiving drove
> her away made her take her laughter and her smiles
> and her softness and her midnight sighs—

Note the hard alliteration of five words beginning with "d" in that fifth line of stanza one— three of them death words—and the three gentler words beginning with "s" in the last two lines of the stanza. These words contrast the man's angry guilt with the woman's innocent charms, more bitterly missed now than ever.

The distinction between her laughter and her smiles is a nice touch. The key thing in this part of the stanza, though, is his admitting to his ongoing drug problem and the dishonesty it entails, along with a death wish signaled by the triple pile-on of "death dead dying". Apparently, it took the loss of his lover to wring this confession out of him.

Then comes the epic profane rant of stanza two, starting with "Fuck Coltrane and music and clouds drifting in the sky / fuck the sea and trees and the sky and birds" (note that this forward slash, and every one used hereafter, was inserted by me to denote a line break). Somewhat counterintuitively, the movement of his rage goes from the particular to the universal: first the icon of Black creativity Coltrane, then all music; first clouds drifting in the sky, then the sky itself. So far all of the things cited are those normally associated with happiness and tranquility. The sea, which was merely implied by the image of a white sandy beach in stanza one, is explicitly told to fuck itself in stanza two, perhaps for not being able to provide its accustomed peace in this time of grievous loss. It's worth noting that Coltrane is the only proper name or proper noun capitalized in the entire poem, outranking Mary, Joseph, Jesus and the author himself, who uses a Cummings-style small "i".

Knight starts to switch it up in line three of this stanza (line 10 of the poem overall) by listing alligators among those creatures that should get fucked. Alligators? Really? Up until this poem, the only thing that ever fucked an alligator was another alligator. Again moving from the specific to the universal, he follows the curse against alligators with "all the animals that roam the earth". Now the litany of things that should be fucked enters high gear with politics and ideology: "fuck marx and mao fuck fidel and nkrumah and / democracy and communism" (lines four and five of stanza two, lines 11 and 12 of the poem overall). He pauses to call out "smack and pot / and red ripe tomatoes" (!) before heading into the home stretch of his rant, from the beginning of line 13 to the end of the poem:

> . . . fuck joseph fuck mary fuck
> god jesus and all the disciples fuck fanon nixon
> and malcolm fuck the revolution fuck freedom fuck
> the whole mothafucking thing
> all i want now is my woman back
> so my soul can sing

I remembered that Kwame Nkrumah was the first President of Ghana, but I had to look up Frantz Fanon, the French West Indian Marxist theorist of decolonization whose work must've been important to Knight. Juxtaposing his name with that of Richard Nixon is one of the few notes of humor in this otherwise bleak poem.

Throughout this work resonates the idea of loneliness as its own kind of prison. As noted in the study by Cassie Premo, Knight often focuses on "the theme of prisons imposed from without (slavery, racism, poverty, incarceration) and prisons from within (addiction, repetition of painful patterns) [which] are countered by the theme of freedom." Knight himself once said, "Ideas are not the source of poetry. For me, it's passion, heart and soul." Few more passionate and soulful poems about the prison of loneliness exist in our language. I believe this poem will have things to say to us about our shared humanity for a long time to come.

Kurt Luchs

Hit and Run

Shit motherfucker you're murdering me!
I wanted to scream, and did,
but no one was there to hear
nor could they have heard
over the roar of his engine
and the whine of mine,
his 18-wheeler drifting into my VW Rabbit
as he drifted off to sleep,
no warning, no turn signal, no horn
on a rainy and foggy Chicago midnight.
His right front wheels
smashed into my left,
bouncing my car into the overpass guard rail
that had me trapped.

Goddamn motherfucking piece of shit!
I bellowed again and again
as the car twirled and slammed back
into his other wheels,
each one the mouth of a Great White
looking to swallow me whole
or drag me under the behemoth,
tearing off hubcaps and side mirrors
like chunks of silver flesh
too tasty to chew properly,
spinning madly, adding vertigo to terror.

Son of a motherfucking bitch!
I gasped as I hit the guard rail again,
rebounding into the truck wheels once more
and landing behind him in the center lane,
finally stopping at a 45-degree angle,
the radiator already steaming,
the car so totaled I had to crawl
out the back hatch on my hands and knees.
I stood there shaking, lightly whiplashed
but otherwise unhurt
and oh so glad to be alive, car be damned.

That motherfucking bastard of a truck driver
kept going (the cops caught him later)
and I didn't care one bit
because while the crash was happening
my life had flashed before my eyes
exactly as they say it does,
and it was not a good life,
not even enough to put on a tombstone.
In that instant my spirit
came out of hibernation
wide-eyed and blinking in astonishment.
So began an awakening
that continues to this day,
every morning since then an unbidden gift
from a mysterious stranger whose face
has yet to emerge from the fog
and the never-ending screech
of giant rubber wheels grinding metal.

GABRIELLE MCAREE

It's Yesterday
Where She Is

I'm starting to forget what you look like, she says, cradling her phone to her ear.

The screen is hot against her skin, pale from spending another summer indoors. She thinks about touching herself to the sound of his voice but doesn't. She's too old for that now. It would be embarrassing, wiping herself off with a Kleenex, burying it at the bottom of the wastebin. Catching her reflection in the mirror afterwards, her cheeks flushed, forehead shiny. She gets out of bed, turns on the stove, and fills the kettle with sink water. Outside, streetlights start to come on. Car lights illuminate. Store fronts flicker. Down the hall, a television blares. A dog barks. Heels pound against her ceiling. She imagines the college girls next door putting on lipstick and pushup bras, hoping to find a trust-fund husband or, at least, a good fuck. She was like that once, eager, desperate enough to constrain her muffin top with a corset. But she found comfort in waffle fries and canned beer; subbed lines of coke out for sitcom reruns; took up knitting. She pulls a loose string out from her t-shirt until it rips off. Where he is, it's morning. People are making coffee and watching the news, ironing their dress shirts, kissing their wives, readying themselves for corporate war. Something about the time difference makes it difficult for her to remember if he has that mustache or not. If she were forced to recall his face at gunpoint, she couldn't do it, though this is probably a defense mechanism.

Just Google me, he says. That's what I do for you.

She types his name into the engine on her computer and drags the mouse over the search button, watching the cursor blink. Technology makes it almost impossible for her to avoid him. He is always a click away, always lingering in her search history. She bites her thumbnail to the bed and turns away from the screen, leaving the page up. She opens her tea cabinet, takes the last bag of earl grey of out the box and discards the cardboard into a blue recycling bin. Tomorrow, she'll have to buy a replacement.

Are you looking at me yet? he asks.

She takes a short, unhappy breath and clicks 'search.' In seconds, hundreds of photographs appear. Most of them shirtless. She scrolls aimlessly waiting for one to appear that she hasn't already seen. We're lucky, she says. Not everyone has 10 million shirtless JPEGs floating around the internet. You should get royalties.

Hm. Last week it was 9 million. I must be trending.

She smiles to herself and then stops, abruptly, as if to censor herself. She looks over her shoulder to make sure no one is watching her, though she knows she is alone. She does this whenever she finds herself thinking of him in public. She would never tell anyone about their relationship. Not her mother, who she is particularly close with, or even her roommate, who buys her dark chocolate when she's on her period. They have a joke relationship. That's what she calls it, and he agrees. Joke relationships are common amongst their age group, their friends. The only people who are married are the people with children, and even they don't seem happy.

She stops on a photograph of him with a skinny blonde woman wearing dark sunglasses. He's turning away from the camera so only his side profile is visible; his hand is on the small of her back. They're laughing at something outside the frame. They look commercially good together, like their relationship alone could conjure a mass following. It brings a sharp pain to her temple. She brings her hands to the crown of her head and applies pressure. She knows she has to say something.

You're not as chiseled as you once were, she finally says. I imagine modern sculptors are disappointed. Not to mention your fans. Do they photoshop you on posters now?

He laughs. Probably. It's my secret McDonald's addiction. I can't kick it.

What would your agent say if he knew?

Oh, I don't know. Probably make me keep a diet journal or something. Do a smoothie cleanse. What are you doing right now?

Making tea.

Oh. He swallows; his voice falling into a character, one she imagines he practices in his full-length mirror. Ok. Are you in your pajamas?

Yeah.

Which ones?

The pink set with the lace.

That's my favorite one.

Yeah. I know.

She studies herself in the reflection of their toaster. She's wearing her dad's old racing t-shirt and a pair of her roommate's flannel sweatpants. She doesn't have the money or the discipline for a pajama set, let alone the silk one in the storefront by work. When she runs out of clean underwear, she steals her roommate's, and if she's desperate, she buys a couple of pairs on clearance. She doesn't wash her face or floss. Being an 'adult' is still a foreign concept to her.

Do you think you'll ever visit me? he asks. Hypothetically. Like, if I were to buy you a plane ticket and pick you up from the airport and pay for all your meals and everything.

She stares at herself until her facial features distort. Her nose floats away from the center of her face and lands on the microwave; her ears, the refrigerator. Hypothetically? she asks. Like if UFOs were real and dinosaurs existed and humans shit gold? Sure, I'd visit you in my private jet in a trench coat with nothing under it.

Yeah? You would?

The tea pot whistles, startling her. She moves it to the warming pad and turns the knob on the stove off. She grabs a dirty mug from the sink without looking at it and drops the tea bag in,

watching intently as it sinks to the bottom. Her hands shake as she lowers them closer and closer to the stove. When she can't bare the heat anymore, she runs them over cold water.

There's no sound on his end, so she takes the phone away from her ear and looks at the screen. They've been on the phone for 2 hours and 27 minutes.

Are you still there or did we disconnect? she asks. She goes over to look at her router. All four lights are green. Hello?

I think I want you to visit me, he says.

Like as a joke? Are we still playing the game?

No, honestly. I want you to get on a plane and come see me.

The last time they saw each other was at his sister's wedding. Two years and three dress sizes ago. They were drunk, or she was drunk, and devastatingly single after getting left for a yoga instructor, again. She doesn't remember if he drank or not. A month later, when she finally got the nerve to take a pregnancy test, she cried when there was only one line.

Jesus, she says, putting her phone back up against her ear. She removes the dishes from the sink and fills it with soapy water. The act of scrubbing old food calms her. Don't be ridiculous, she crows.

What? Does it bother you? Me wanting to see you?

No, it's just predictable. Like, of course you want to see me until you see me.

I don't know what that means.

She smacks her head against the cabinet, a cherry-stained wood that's peeling, and lets it hang there. She wants to do something permanent to alter her appearance but can't think of anything immediate. Last year, she cut off her hair with kitchen scissors in a maniac fit, gave herself middle school bangs. She steadies her grip on the phone and says: I don't see the point in discussing it if it's not going to happen.

Or I could come to you, he says, his voice pre-pubescent. She hears clicking from his keyboard. I could book a flight right now.

And what's that going to accomplish? Are you going to put a ring on my finger, Will? Make a modest woman out of me? Christ. Be practical.

I could. I mean, I would. You know I would. I would never ask you to be modest.

She dumps her undrunk tea into the sink, washes the mug, and puts it upside down on the drying rack. There's nothing else to clean. The dishes are done, scrubbed to shine; the counters wiped; the rugs wrung out in the hallway. The oven clock ticks towards 8:00 pm. Her roommate will be home soon.

It's not that easy. Look, I've got to get going. Emily and I are going to a pub to celebrate her getting fired.

Emily got fired? Why?

Workplace harassment or something, I don't know. They're buying out her contract.

Oh. She was harassed or she did the harassing?

I don't know. Does it matter?

I guess not. Ok. Well, have fun.

Yeah. I'll talk to you later.

She holds the freezer door open and sticks her head inside. Every time she talks to him, it takes her hours to resort back to her normal self. She cocoons in her bedroom, balled up in an old sweater with the curtains drawn, until she remembers she is a real person with medical records and rent payments and not some plaything with plastic breasts. Emily thinks she needs to see a psychiatrist, or at least, get addicted to over-the-counter medicine. If she had a habit, say, a coke problem, then her suffering could be named, pointed to, justified.

Wait. He clears his throat. Jess?

She pinches the excess fat on her thighs, not remembering how it got there. What?

I do love you, you know.

She molds her tongue to the roof of her mouth and closes her eyes, dropping the phone to her side. She never should have gone to his sister's wedding. She should have spent the money on something unnecessary, like a boob job or latex surgery, something tangible, like Botox. Her bridesmaid's dress alone was one week's salary. The flight, another. And she's only seen his sister a couple times since graduating. It's not like they send each other long voicemails with intimate details about their lives or anything. She was a filler bridesmaid, an old friend forgets to wish her a happy birthday, someone to even out the bridal party in pictures. Yeah, Will. I know you love me, she says, rubbing her eyes in a hard, circular motion. I love you too, ok?

Ok. Uh. She hears his breath catch on the other end. She wonders if he's standing or sitting; if he's wearing a dress shirt or if he's still in his underwear. Is it weird that I want to thank you? he asks, earnestly.

No. It's not.

Keys jingle outside their door. The lock unlashes followed by Emily's breathless voice. She bellows: Oh for fuck's sake, this fucking door.

She slips out of Emily's pajama pants, throws them in the hamper, and pulls down the racing t-shirt over her underwear. Will, she says. I've got to go.

When she hangs up, he sits down on the bed to close his eyes, lean his head against his headboard, his phone slack in his hands. He lets himself think of her. Of Jess. Of her shoebox apartment, the red refrigerator, the dirty clothes, that teapot. Unzipping her bridesmaid dress. He doesn't notice when his phone falls to the ground, the screen cracking, or the knock at his door. He imagines Jess putting on a pair of jeans and a t-shirt, something casual, something unwashed. Sipping warm beer at a pub she doesn't like, straining to hear Emily over bad music, smiling politely at the man who pays her tab. The sun is up now, hanging in the sky like a toenail. His agent will be calling soon, telling where to go, when. Where she is, it's yesterday.

Julian Stannard

The Lentil Chronicles

The portrait of the un-named man comes in great part through the eyes and ears of the philosopher lentil, or lentil *philosophe*, the organizing editorial voice, who, it would seem, had plenty of opportunity to observe and ponder. It's calculated *The Lentil Chronicles* were written over a handful of weeks which in 'Lentil Time' is equivalent to several decades. It's difficult to be certain about the historical moment. Scholars see these chronicles as a testament to one of the great epochs of the legume, a tantalizing insight into a culture that has endured millennia, almost all of which remains undocumented, especially from the point of view of the lentil.

There are mysteries and there are mysteries. It's exhilarating to learn the common red lentil—characteristically distinguished from its yellow, green and brown kinsfolk by a 'split' veneer and an orange hue—has demonstrated a capacity to communicate in a written language other than its own. The calligraphy is exquisite. Jane Austen's 'six inches of ivory', in comparison, is gargantuan, even vulgar. The culture of atoms, typically, has been in the hands of scientists, though it remains instructive to recall the work of the Roman poet Lucretius. If the splitting of the atom represented the acne of scientific endeavor, the split lentil has been largely ignored in literary circles.

The interpretation of *The Lentil Chronicles* draws on linguists and literary theorists from some of the country's leading universities, close readers with a forensic aptitude. A debt of gratitude is owed to Professor Smallbone from the University of East Anglia whose unfailing modesty belies extraordinary scholarship as well as an emotional intelligence of the highest order.

Thanks to advances in technology the calligraphy has been amplified to human scale or, in popular parlance, 'blown up'; the verb 'blow', in fact, resonating in its various iterations and conjugations with the history of the lentil itself. The text is full of surprises. One irresistible aphorism, a squib perhaps, a last-ditch supplication, beseeches Aeolus, Keeper of the Winds, who, we subsequently learn, was not averse to an occasional bowl of lentil soup.

The clarity of the writing is startling; Professor Lupo from the University of Palermo used the word *limpido*. It now seems clear the chronicles were written in several hands—merchants, seafarers, cartographers, refugees, ne'er-do-wells. There are single words or 'utterances' from the *hoi polloi*, and the lowest lentils of the low as well as more polished pieces from a Mandarin elite. It appears there was at least one travelling poet, if not a group of Troubadours whose genealogy reaches back, it would seem, to Languedoc .

There has been much debate as to whether the lentil *philosophe* might (himself) be one of the poets; the jury is still out, and readers who have followed media attention regarding the manuscript will know that a season of conferences has been given over to this question as well as several contiguous matters. One commentator has made the case, not without mischief, that the excitement generated by *The Lentil Chronicles* has something in common with the passionate response to that great hoaxer James McPherson. Unlike *Ossian*—that eighteenth century conceit—the existence of the *Chronicles* is welded in literary truth and verifiable fact.

The gendering of the lentils has been brought into focus not only by an array of personal pronouns but also by that declaration—a single line no less— 'I LENTIL, THROBBING BETWEEN TWO LIVES', one of the few occasions, in fact, when capital letters are used.

Several French feminists have taken up cudgels on behalf of *Écriture Lentille*; other critics have argued these fragments are emblematic of non-binary hyper-liberated inscription. Although most of the 'protagonists' in the manuscript take on a male persona—this might have been learnt behavior or simply a mimetic response to the materials in the house—there is a distinctly female section. These voices come in large part from those lentils which remained trapped inside the bag—wives mostly—who chant a choral lament for their wandering partners who have been scattered throughout the house and beyond and show no sign of returning. This section of the manuscript has been called 'The Book of Lentil Lamentations'—one striking if simple strophe cries out 'Deliver us from these poly(methylene) walls!'

The Boadicea of Second Wave Feminism Germaine Greer, whose face now bears the scars of many battles, has contributed to the debate by employing her culinary skills. Taking a large pot hanging on the wall of her kitchen Professor Greer set about making a lentil casserole and, once it had cooled, she placed it squarely in the garden. Locals were delighted to see the early arrival of Barn Swallows and soon, no doubt attracted by the nascent hum of the casserole, birds of all type, from far and near, great and small, alighted in the professor's garden. A red-bottomed woodpecker announced Greer's cooking was better than any number of fat balls and over the course of the day the legumes were ingested, excreted, regurgitated, spilt as the birds flew away in all directions. Hence the lentils embarked on another campaign of 'neo-colonial' expansion. 'The gift which keeps on giving' announces one lentil with mischievous brio.

The *Chronicles* are, by nature, fragmentary and heuristic and they are beset by contingency and happenstance. Professor Smallbore has posited that in many instances 'the lentils are thinking on their feet' and sometimes, as it were, 'writing on the hoof'. Smallbone maintains the writing demonstrates both spontaneity and agility. As such their literary output is charged with such a voltage of creativity that any lingering sympathy for Cartesian Dualism is deconstructed once and for all.' Her thesis is broad in scope, if germane. The chroniclers have not only finessed the environmental debate, but they also have, un-likely revolutionaries, up-ended established Anthropocene narratives. Leaders of the major faiths, including the Pontiff, have remained tight-lipped about the theological implications.

Professor Finkelstein, his disquisition both delightful and rigorous, recognizes that some lentils have a gift for riddle making and much of his almost completed monograph has been given over to identifying and adumbrating various examples scattered across the oeuvre. Sometimes dissonant, sometimes mellifluous, sometimes colloquial, sometimes high-minded, sometimes demotic, and sometimes quasi-erotic, this suite of riddles has both an accumulative and fugal effect. Like the writing elsewhere in the manuscript they display humour in the face of adversity. Some of the riddles have remained—as yet—un-cracked: 'Lord of the Bathroom, you've lost your prong, your nymphs unwashed, who are you now dude? What have you become?'

The lentil *philosophe* himself, herself, themselves, has provided various details about the unnamed man and the domestic environment in which the lentils found themselves. Much of this is fascinating and the reader is placed in a tantalizing space in which the man makes his way distractedly through his day oblivious of the parallel lives of these adventurer lentils, these Lilliputian legumes, these tiny Troubadours, existing and sometimes flourishing in the crevices and corners of the house. The Dog Episode is another matter. Little more than a walk on part, the canine becomes an unwished for *Deus ex Machina*, or as one lentil joker puts it, 'rather like some god leaping out of a car'.

The chroniclers, it seems clear, have been both 'nurtured' and discombobulated by the house. It would appear the man had peopled his home with books, notebooks, newspapers, diaries, sheets of paper various, typewriters and an assortment of ageing computers. A small handful of lentils found themselves lodged in the channels of a keyboard and showed a commendable receptiveness to digital reality. Professor Smallbore makes the bold claim that at least one lentil managed to look up the history of the *Lens Culinaris* on Wikipedia.

The man, it would seem, would spend hours with a book close to his face and the lentil *philosophe* noted that whilst he looked at it, as if 'he were admiring himself in a great river', he would 'oftentimes make handwritten notations' both in the book itself and in one of the many 'exercising books' that had taken up residency in the house. Or he would write on 'scraps of paper' which not only regularly shifted location, but which moved freely between rooms—outriders, 'whippersnappers', free-wheeling thingamajigs—which slowly but surely inserted themselves into 'that great vortex of word-pumping chaos', as if, the *philosophe* continues, the lentils had been sprung from the kitchen cupboard to be 'scattered far and wide into the heart of darkness'.

Professor Finkelstein notes with satisfaction several lentils were, in fact, discovered among the pages of Conrad's great novel which suggests the lentils had ways of communicating between themselves, as it were, of monitoring an awareness of their own Inter-Lenticchial relationships, as well as making some effort to map their whereabouts in the uncharted regions of the house. An examination of the phone's billing records reveals that not only was there a sharp spike in expenditure in this period there was evidence of international numbers that had no bearing with typical usage and which the man has no recollection whatsoever of contacting or having the remotest desire to be in contact with.

Interestingly, comments made by the *philosophe* indicate that he'd, in fact, had previous experience of observing human activity from close quarters. Comparisons are duly made and there are moments when the lentil reveals something which might be construed as empathy. The *philosophe* notes the man would live in 'a great palaver of books' and 'sxrabbling' [sic] and sxrobbling' [sic] and for days on end (years of 'Lentil Time') and then, without further ado, 'open the door to wind gusts and step forth into a world of magpies', in effect making the lentils the unofficial guardians of the house. On one such occasion the man ventured to a post office, we might allow ourselves to speculate he had a manuscript of his own. It appears that back in the house Marvin Gaye's 'What's Going On?' had been left on replay which galvanized a group of lentils with musical inclinations. Professor Boil's seminal paper 'The Hermeneutic Lentil' demonstrates the music prompted a gentle swaying on the part of the legumes now held up in the sitting room, and in response to the music several enthusiasts decided to form themselves into a 'kumquat', which Boil subsequently suggests is a 'rather laudable misspelling' of 'quintet'. We learn, in fact, numbers were integral to an emerging lentil consciousness.

It was, it ought to be said, on another occasion that having gone forth and later returning, the man came back with A SAUSAGE DOG and this addition to the household, albeit temporary, wreaked havoc on the diaspora.

It is evident that the *philosophe* and his fellow literati, in close proximity to the many texts in the house, handwritten or otherwise, were able to recognize patterns and mathematical sequences. Several lentils have written quatorzains. Professor Smallbone argues these might be viewed as 'sonnets manqués', suggesting that the man had been experimenting , *inter alia*, with traditional forms. The most eye-grabbing of these split lentil 'Imitations' begins 'Shall I compare thee to a Tarka Dhal '?

How some lentils became sandwiched between the pages of certain books rather than others is less a matter of conjecture and more an indication of the man's reading habits. It is irrefutable, however, that some enterprising lentils having become accustomed to their new environment and seemingly growing in confidence were able to propel themselves forward and sideways and painstakingly shuffle across the bookshelves, and further afield, as if by choice. There are literary implications. Professor Finkelstein maintains that lentils which had once been among the pages of *L'Etranger* were later found among the page of *La Peste*, suggesting that existential concerns were, for some lentils, important. Beckettian moments too. Having been embroiled in *Waiting for Godot*, renamed on the back cover in bold lentil hand, not without chutzpah, *Waiting For Supper*, the selfsame legume was later found engaging with *Krapp's Last Tape*.

Dead Souls, as far as the lentils are concerned, must be deemed a success. They respond sympathetically to Gogol's humour and detailed accounts of Russian feasting. It appears the *philosophe* was able to conclude that a bag of lentils was not unlike a cathedral of dead souls, a plastic purgatory, if not a circle of hell. After which the quickening realization that having escaped their poly(methylene) incarceration they had been brought back to life, a Lazarus moment on an unimaginable scale, and along with this epiphany various reflections, on the part of the *philosophe* one presumes, regarding The Ever So Long Twentieth Century.

John Ashbery's *Self-Portrait in a Convex Mirror* is worth a couple of sentences. Having taken lodgings in the middle section of the collection several lentils found themselves 'catapulted' to the bathroom. It was a region of strange smells and 'twangling' sounds. The man ran a bath and once it was full to the brim he slid carefully into it with Ashbery's *Self-Portrait* in his right hand, using his left to flick though the pages, foamy bathwater spilling over the edge. Several lentils fell at once into the water for a long soak and for some, alas, a slow drowning, and only later, when the plug had been pulled and the un-clean water sucked into a domestic underworld could the final tally of ruination and resilience be observed. Two damp lentils found themselves marooned on the side of the bathtub, where they bedded down doggedly for the weekend (the best part of a decade in 'Lentil Time'.) If the now clean man had made a study of the soapy bathtub he would have seen these words etched into the dwindling bank of foam I Hear The Voices That Won't be Drowned.

After bathing and reading the poems in a leisurely way the man stood naked in front of the shaving mirror. Several lentils were hidden in the forest of his chest and a couple more had found a nesting place further down below but more significantly if the man were not so short sighted he would have noticed his beard was flecked with orange foot soldiers. It was exactly at this moment these tenacious legumes saw a 'copy' of themselves in the mirror and they enjoyed a Lacanian moment of self-realization: 'The soul establishes itself. / But how far can it swim out through the eyes / And still return safely to its nest?'

Of all the works the lentils had the opportunity to engage with the most challenging was Jacques Derrida's *Of Grammatology*. There is evidence to suggest that the text exercised the lentil *philosophe* and his more educated companions a great deal. Professors Smallbone and Finkelstein are agreed 'the man with notebooks' carried *Of Grammatology* from room to room in a rather fevered way for several days (a great number of years in 'Lentil

Time') which meant that the split legumes trapped among its pages and oftentimes ejected as the pages were turned, and on one occasion when the book was thrown across the room in frustration, experienced a kinetic force as well as an intellectual charge. There appear to have been among the lentil intelligentsia a series of symposia to thrash out the knotty complexities of Deconstructionism.

Derrida' passages on masturbation caused a great deal of consternation. It appears some lentils experienced Onanistic desires, thinking of their partners still lingering in the kitchen cupboard. Or they yearned for the other half of their split selves, nothing less than narcissistic lust. In fact they were able to comprehend without difficulty Derrida's postulations on 'absence' yet although they put their hearts and souls into collective acts of frottage, a history of living cheek by jowl made this a relatively easy task, they never achieved the outcome they were hoping for. On one occasion, we gather, they rubbed against each other whilst listening to James Brown's 'Get On Up—I Feel Like A Sex Machine', which must have been playing on the radio. The lentil *philosophe* eventually declared that Derrida's 'masturbation' was another word for 'mastication'—a good solution in effect—namely a deferred pleasure in which the food is held up and teased in the mouth in anticipation of that final act of consummation (or swallowing); and hence a realization that plentitude and fulfillment were always on the other side of the horizon.

It is surely right to conclude this section by focusing on that heart-stopping discovery by Professor Smallbone, a discovery which has been compared with the unearthing of Tutankhamun in 1922 [I PHAROH, THROBBING BETWEEN TWO LIVES.] It demonstrates the lentils were able to transcribe and transliterate and communicate on a variety of surfaces, including (putatively) various digital platforms, and it shows that if some lentils were little more than curious scribes, the lentil *philosophe* and his coterie were able to unabashedly take on an authorial role (*pace* Roland Barthes) that reveals both sentience and consciousness. Professor Boil's unfinished paper 'The Lentil Mind' explores this further.

On her hands and knees, a position that Professor Smallbone assumed more frequently in the final stages of the project, the scholar from East Anglia examined with forensic scrupulosity the floor boards, the Bokhara rugs, that area beneath the sofa bed and in between the grooves of various armchairs, along the alleyways of kitchen cupboards, several drawers of spoons and miscellanea; and then she climbed the 'terraced mountain slopes', with their 'near invisible groves' which took her to the second floor and the bathroom, previously mentioned, and the master bedroom, and therein a vast wardrobe, the lining of a suitcase, trouser pockets, and the great double bed (she'd asked permission to rummage between those tired sheets). She was looking for any flame-haired Pict, any lingering Japanese soldier still hidden in the jungle unaware the war was over and lost.

After The Dog Episode and Magda's 'Sucking Machine'—described by one flailing lentil as the Nakba—which she brought over to the house at the end of every month, the lentil period, as we know it, had come to an end. It was now Professor Smallbone found it, more brilliant than any Banksy, an act of completion as well as an act of self-effacement, a spectral reckoning, an epistemological implosion. There on the skirting board in that unmistakable lentil hand she read:

THERE IS NOTHING OUTSIDE THE TEXT
ONLY A GLANCE IN THE WRONG DIRECTION

THE BEGINNING

'I cannot make it cohere'

When the careless, man, the lumbering man, the bearded man, the myopic man, the big-boned man, the 'great liberator' took the large bag of unopened lentils from the kitchen cupboard it was that most modest day of the week—Tuesday. The warp and weft of modesty hung in the air. It was mid-morning and Woman's Hour was chuntering on, un-listened to, in some other room.

He was unaware he was about to open the curtains onto a theatrical spectacle bigger than any Broadway Show. Readers will have noted this section has been called 'The Beginning' but there's always a beginning before the beginning. In the beginning was the word, but as the lentil *philosophe* writes 'What was in the recipe *before* the word?'

The bag of lentils had lived quietly in the kitchen cupboard for a long time. From the *Chronicles* we learn it was called 'the epoch of unending bondage', or 'the epoch of perpetual longueurs', or 'the epoch of lachrymose supplication'. Imprisonment in a plastic fortress was both a comfort and a curse. For circa two years the lentils rubbed shoulders with prisoners from far and wide. They could see their chastened inmates through the great window of their poly (methylene) jail. According to the chroniclers the kitchen cupboard, at various moments, contained: No Hurry Chicken Curry Mix, packets of opened and abandoned rice, Oolong Tea Bags, Whole Jeera Cumin Seeds, Aloo Gobi and Cauliflower Spice, bags of pasta, some unopened, various shapes, various sizes; stock cubes, cinnamon sticks ('poor man's cigars') , a bag of ground white pepper, Lem Sip (seasonal flow), desiccated coconut, Aubergine Blush, dried chilis (crushed), and a jar of RIDICULOUSLY LAZY GINGER never opened, allowing the ginger to become lazier and yet lazier still.

We learn the lentils, an industrious people, were bemused and intrigued by the concept of sloth. It would appear that a small but not insignificant group of split legumes argued they might themselves embrace the Alakefic life. These lentils slipped slowly to the bottom of the bag and fell into a state of inactivity, what the *philosophe* described as 'Lentil Quietism'.

The coffee zone of the cupboard, in contrast, was as frenetic as Heathrow Airport, whose comings and goings were the envy of the lentil folk. There were also, quoting from the *Chronicles*, 'several bawdy bottles of upturned ketch-up' and if this wasn't bad enough there was yet another layer of melancholy.

The man of letters, if that's how we should call him, shopped on the corner. Many pleasant conversations took place with the keeper of the Corner Shop and over time he noticed almost everything he bought had gone beyond its expiry date. The shop owner said on one occasion, not without a touch of pride, 'We don't have expiry dates in my country' and thereafter, in the man's mind, the shop on the corner was 'the corner shop without temporal restrictions' which allowed him to wander through time and through countries as if he were Marco Polo with all the delights of novelty without the discomfort of travel.

When he came to buy the bag of red lentils, a fairly large bag—2 kg/4.4lbs—the shop keeper proclaimed 'And for you my friend, half price!' That bag of lentils had never been expensive and now that the price had been reduced it must have been one of the cheapest bags in the country. When the man put it in the cupboard he almost wanted to smile, or weep, his emotions strangely stirred. The lentils had lived in that bag for several decades—'Lentil Time'—before beginning another period of captivity.

The kitchen cupboard was not without touches of glamour. The lentils noted with awe and a touch of schadenfreude that among the Tom, Dick and Harry's of the cupboard folk there was a cylindrical pink box called The Poachers Relish, Perfect Spread on Toast, Crackers and Blinis (best before, see side of pack . . .), and even more luxurious, even rather louche, a lean green tin of sardines with a brace of lemons in the corner evoking balmy evenings on some foreign shore. This was the first time the lentils had encountered the French language.

Sardines Préparées à la Main à L'Huile d'Olive Vierge Extra. And at the top of the tin—in royal red—it said Depuis 1959 à Concarneau followed by LES MOUETTES D'ARVOR. The lentil *philosophe* had written, one of his first observations perhaps, 'Our little heads break through the clouds of unknowing ....'

On another occasion, a Thursday perhaps, there was a further addition. A brown tin of ORGANIC CHICKPEAS, MADE WITH LOVE FOR THE PLANET! I ought to say none of the above came from the Corner Shop. They were birthday presents from a faraway sister and they had a certain swagger as they looked at their fellow prisoners *de haut en bas*.

If the lentils were impressed by what they saw they also thought (wrongly) that if their imprisonment behind plastic had been a cruelly punitive sentence those tinned and/or glass walls were an Alcatraz from which the sardines, the chickpeas, the lazy ginger et al would never escape. And this provided a degree of comfort as they watched themselves ignored like Cinderella for lentil decades, as the man put in his hand for this and for that but never for them, meek wretched sheepish split legumes . . .

Yet some mostly insignificant Saturday the illusion was shattered. Those slightly louche sardines were freed from Alcatraz, as if it were Judgement day *avant la lettre*, called to stand (or lie soaked in oil) before the Great Sardine. The hand of the man reached into the cupboard and the green tin was plucked out as if it were a vole seized by a bird of prey. The man, in haste, didn't bother closing the cupboard door which meant thousands of lentils witnessed the terrible, quasi-mystical, reckoning.

The once proud tin, now on its back, said *Au revoir Au revoir* to swagger. No lush green here, no balmy lemons, no royal red, only dull grey metal. And the lentils were amazed to see some built in opening mechanism, biding its time yet not without purpose. The man opened the tin like a sarcophagus.

And for a moment it was as if Concarneau offered up its streets, its markets, its clatter, its citrus warmth, its oh là là and just as quickly as the gift of life appeared it slipped away, like a distant, un-bearable ache.

Sardines which had once swum in the rocky waters of Brittany now found themselves on the south coast of England, about to be spread unceremoniously across a piece of toast. *Vive L'Entente Cordial!*

That modest Tuesday which I referred to above came at last. The train of thought which caused the man to reach for the bag of lentils is difficult to pin down with certitude: a cooking programme on the television? A conversation with his Shri-Lankan friend in Jericho? He'd come back from the Corner Shop with a cucumber 'only two days beyond its expiry date', one of the finest cucumbers he'd ever bought. He was wearing his blue coat with missing buttons and capacious pockets. He was wearing his mustard yellow corduroy trousers which had survived many human years, whose left pocket boasted a small hole which meant that sometimes loose change ran down his leg and spiraled its way into the corner of the corner shop—a down payment for those many purchases that were yet to take place.

He'd finished with *Of Grammatology*. He was now holding a bag of lentils and contemplating how he should go about opening it. It was like a baby's head, a baby sprouting an outcrop of reddish hair. In order to pin down the facts as accurately as possible it should be recorded that just as he was considering his options—brute force, scissors, a combination of both, or, the easiest option, and in hindsight the best option, putting the bag back into the cupboard unopened—there was a rattle at the window. There, on the other side of the glass, was Lady Macbeth.

Lady Macbeth was the neighborhood cat who brought you her catch at the drop of a hat— usually mice, sometimes birds, occasionally a rat. The man, that Tuesday, wasn't in the mood for Lady Macbeth so he shouted, gesticulating at the same time with one of the hands he'd freed from the bag 'BUGGER OFF, GO AND SEE MISS CRUIKSHANK !' Miss Cruickshank was rather old and as might be expected she adored cats, even this one.

The encounter with Lady Macbeth took only a few seconds but it distracted the man from the task in hand. It was as if by shouting at the cat he'd been pumped with adrenaline so he pulled at the top of the bag with both hands forcefully and the very thing he'd feared might happen happened. The bag split, almost in two, and an avalanche of lentils bounced off the worktop, as if in slow motion, onto the kitchen floor, not a few of them landing in a couple of drawers half open and many others scattering in all directions across the kitchen. This was the beginning of the lentil diaspora.

'Fuck! the man said and then again 'fuck , fuck , fuck.' He'd liberated himself from *Of Grammatology* and this is what he'd got in return—a heaving sea of dried legumes spreading and throbbing across the kitchen, some spilling into the long corridor that linked the sitting room at the front of the house to the utility room at the back.

 He leant against the wall and lit a cigarette. He watched some mauled rodent twitching on the windowsill. Some part of his brain was hardwiring an instruction to his personal in-tray 'Don't buy lentils again— I don't like them much anyway . . .' If this had been a small spillage he would have turned on his heels post-haste and dealt with it later, if at all. This, however, was a deluge.

He finished the cigarette and went to look for the long-handled broom that lived in the cupboard under the stairs. Although he walked with a certain amount of gingerly care he picked up several lentils on the bottoms of his shoes and dispatched them to various outposts of the corridor; some of them lone riders, some of them in pairs, some of them in little groups of three. This was the lentils' first experience of the great river—the Amazon, the Mississippi, the Mekong—which flowed uninterruptedly, with its own primeval rhythms, between the back and front of the house. It was now, in effect, that some of these lentils, like Vasco di Gama, like Columbus, like Captain Cook, began their voyages of discovery: journeys fraught with danger, surprise and yearning. One lentil lyricist compared this drift with a felucca wandering down the Nile: marvelous visions unfolding on its banks, Nubian instruments caught mouthwateringly in the breeze.

The man's brush pushed a great pile of lentils into a heap, a holding pen, and then he realized that the dust pan, for reasons he couldn't remember, was in the bedroom, so he climbed the stairs depositing several lentils on the terraces, and the corridor on the second floor, as well as in his own befuddled bedroom. If one could have reduced oneself to the size of a lentil, if only in the mind's eye, one might have seen these plucky flotillas, sails dipped in the salty breeze, Leviathan fish swimming alongside, and one might just have made out the Nina, Pinta and Santa Maria in the wind-flap of that fateful crossing. The colonization of the house had begun.

The bulk of the lentils was chucked in the kitchen bin. For these unfortunates the liberation had been a cruel illusion, the briefest taste of freedom before an incarceration worse than anything previously experienced. For these woe-begone lentils the red sea which had promised so much never 'opened up' like the Old Testament miracle. There was no delivery from bondage. The man had eaten fish two days earlier (fish on Sunday!) and the bones of a sea bass jostled among the detritus, the kitchen cast offs, the accumulating rot. For a split lentil this was worse than any vision Hieronimo Bosch might have conjured up.

It is argued the *philosophe* may well have been responsible in some way for a villanelle called 'Vicissitudes'. Professor Smallbone maintains it encapsulates that balance between restriction and freedom lost, alluding knowingly to Elizabeth Bishop's 'I lost two cities, lovely ones. And, vaster'. This is one of the *Chronicles*' most sophisticated poems.

Yet if the bulk of lentils were now in the kitchen bin and soon to be dropped into a larger receptacle outside the house (green-coloured) and then taken in a lorry to a 'death camp' faraway and out of sight—one can only surmise how many individuals wriggled free on those brutal journeys, and good luck to them—the careless man was not yet aware that the capacious pockets of his blue coat were full of lentils and that the pockets of his mustard yellow corduroys were similarly engorged including the pocket with the hole which during the next few days provided a reliable escape route—'the lentil run'—which meant those 'little people' were trickled out across the rooms and corridors and tables and chairs of that book-muddled house.

Some found themselves in distant corners which Gaston Bachelard describes as 'that most sordid of havens' yet the Frenchman continues 'the corner deserves to be examined. To withdraw into the corner is undoubtedly a meagre expression. But despite its meagerness, it boasts something of great antiquity, something psychologically primitive.' Professor Finkelstein was almost beside himself when he found several lentils sandwiched between well-thumbed pages of *The Poetics of Space* and in the margins of that book he came across, in perfect hand, **The Galactic Lentils!**—alongside a pleasing doodle of Apollo 11.

Although the man was pleased enough with his lentil clearing operation in the first instance he was discombobulated to see the appearance of 'orange hieroglyphics' dotted far and wide about the house. He took up the brush again and did a little desultory sweeping here and here but any movement on his part meant more lentils leaked out of his pockets or slipped down his trouser leg. And when he sat down he provided the perfect opportunity for further break outs: lentils sliding between cushions, hiding in the upholstery, or melting into a shadowy un-policed hinterland.

He was beginning to feel like Sisyphus. He'd thought of calling Magda but Magda was so busy nowadays and somewhat to his embarrassment he owed her quite a lot of money. Although we don't know how the man earned from his efforts we know his toiling wasn't lucrative. There was no central heating in the house and Easter still a good month away and oftentimes the man wore his blue coat and oftentimes he took it off and his mustard yellow trousers, notwithstanding the hole in the pocket, were warm and comfortable. He wore them for a fortnight before realizing they were unapologetic lentil-carriers.

If the initial clean up that Tuesday morning was like the building of the Maginot Line, the wearing of his blue coat and yellow cords was the Ardennes through which the Germans took Europe by surprise by sending in their troops and tanks. The lentil invasion was an act of stealth and we haven't yet noted how in that initial outpouring, the great deluge, several lentils found safe harbor in the man's beard and several attached themselves to his woolen jumper. After a few days he was no longer surprised to wake up in the morning to find legumes relaxing in his bed without a care in the world.

If the man were not a rich man, he was a busy one. There were books to read and reviews to write and deadlines to meet and although at first he was surprised to find the occasional lentil hiding among the leaves of a book, the surprise gave way to tolerance and even moments of kindness. The empathy for the man shown by the lentil *philosophe* was, in some degree, reciprocated. If the man had known his writerly activities were creating a parallel world of literary endeavor he would have fallen off his chair. The bemusement regarding their growing presence soon gave way to other concerns. Somewhat rashly he'd agreed to look after a friend's dog and now that day was approaching.

Fearful of breaching the rules of good taste, I ought to return, albeit briefly, to the lentils' sexual lives. We noted that frottage came naturally, the act enlivened one morning by listening to James Brown. We noted, too, that despite their best efforts the lentils never arrived at that transcendental, if solipsistic, moment described by Jacques Derrida in *Of Grammatology*. The lentil *philosophe* was delighted, therefore, when he found himself lodged one afternoon among the pages of the King James Bible. More precisely he found himself in the Book of Genesis:

And God blessed them, and God said unto them, Be fruitful, and multiply, and replenish the earth, and subdue it: and have dominion over the fish of the sea, and over the fowl of the air . . .

We know from the *Chronicles* that the *philosophe* convened an extraordinary meeting and after two days of passionate discussion his kinsfolk realized with sudden clarity this godly fiat was directed at them. It was a sign! As far as they were concerned the earth was the house in which they now resided and furthermore the missives sent from those lentil explorers on the great river confirmed the appearance of both fish and fowl. 'Be fruitful and multiply' became their call to arms and although the process of lentil procreation is now being studied by cultural biologists at the University of Oxford, Professor Finkelstein is convinced that the biblical instruction created a spiritual imperative which underscored the lentils' proliferation. He has made the case, somewhat contentiously, that the lentils were graced with 'an ejaculate which was mysteriously infused with the immaculate.'

ALMOST THE END

'I still can't make it cohere'

The Interactive Lentil Chronicles Exhibition at the Ashmolean has been deemed a success; the panel of Smallbone, Finkelstein and Boil on hand to answer questions. And what a panel! The curatorship of the exhibition was not without complications, not least because Magda's 'Sucking Machine' removed many of the scraps of paper on which the lentils had written their work, not to mention the lentils themselves. Fortunately the *philosophe*'s notations, observations and apercus, dotted generously around the house, helped the team contextualize the writings and piece together the wider narrative.

Professor Smallbone has succeeded in creating a facsimile of what might be called the ur-chronicles, yet it requires a skilled reader and a further edition with copious accompanying notes is in the pipeline. Readers will see that if the lentils wrote mostly in the Roman alphabet they also experimented with ideograms, pictograms and peculiar hieroglyphics. Smallbone has called the project 'something of a jigsaw puzzle.' Her efforts to trace the last remaining lentils were compounded by the visit of Maxine, the twelve-year-old bitch— those twelve years entailing a great number of years for both humans and lentils alike. Though Maxine only slept at the man's house for three nights she had, it would seem, a Teutonic ruthlessness when it came to hunting down lentils who had hidden themselves away. Her long tongue found them out, those uncooked legumes settling uneasily in her stomach. It was only when she was returned to her owner that the dog's insides staged an out and out rebellion and he was horrified to see she'd used the kitchen floor to relieve her troubled bowels, hence expelling those half-digested lentils into an altogether different sphere and who knows what stories are now unfolding in that place.

Professor Smallbone's last-ditch efforts to evacuate and bring to safety those heroic lentils lingering in the man's house, we will never be sure whether the *philosophe* were among them, weren't in vain. If the reader feels they have suspended their disbelief quite enough she must gird her loins once again. The lentils which Professor Smallbone brought back to the Ashmolean laboratory had a charisma which seized the imagination of the studio engineers. Consider that recording of Tennyson's 'The Charge of the Light' Brigade on wax cylinder in 1890. Surely it's not unreasonable to imagine the Victorian poet would have written a similar poem to commemorate the lentils' acts of courage, their ultimate sacrifice: 'Theirs not to reason why/Theirs but to do and die.'

Running auditory-neurological tests the engineers found that the small jar of lentils which Professor Smallbone had brought to them was producing a sound of such high frequency the human ear could flap till the end of time without apprising itself of the content. By a process of 'auditory capture', or 'acoustic down scaling', the team of technicians together with Professor Smallbone, hovering about like Teresa of Ávila, were dumbfounded to hear the lentils had not only learnt how to write in English they could speak it, and some of them could even sing it. In effect this small jar of beleaguered legumes was able to leave an oral testimony, somewhat fragmentary, of their time in the man's house.

He seemingly led a rather solitary life which meant many conversations were carried out on the telephone so the lentils caught snippets of literary bricolage and oftentimes unconnected gossip, some of it rather salacious. Yet the lentils were exposed a great deal to the radio—Farming Today, Desert Island Discs, Book at Bed Time, the Shipping Forecast (quite useful for those lentil seafarers), Sailing By (their version of the latter has distinctly Shostakovian accents.) Among the sounds that emanated from that small jar, like microscopic parrots their skills lie mostly in imitation, there was a rendering, almost two minutes long, and slightly off key, of Frank Sinatra's 'Come Fly with Me ': 'There's a bar in far Bombay/ Come fly with me, let's fly away!'

The quality of the recording is a little thin and like the rescued texts themselves the Ashmolean Exhibition has been—necessarily—'Time Sensitive'. Ultimately *The Lentil Chronicles* are a profoundly evanescent experience. Nevertheless, the writings of Smallbone, Finkelstein and Boil have created an archive which not only has an air of authority but one that will doubtless be opened up again with no little excitement should there be further developments.

The lumbering man, the myopic man, the bearded man, the 'great liberator' has likewise provided corroborative evidence from his own recollections and now that he knows his former house mates were literary grafters he seems to be experiencing a kind of love sickness for the vanished legumes. He peeps under chairs and cushions in the hope of finding some dreamy straggler.

The haphazard, de-stabilizing dynamic of *The Lentil Chronicles* means the facsimile—Dionysian rather than Apollonian—is best appreciated by deliberating upon the many papers, not to mention monographs, that engage with the manuscript, and which will become available in the course of time. Below are some of the more substantial fragments from the lentil oeuvre. The writing has been standardized for the sake of clarity. The disappearing nature of the Chronicles means readers are advised to read in haste, and with an open heart.

DREAM-Y-O

MY HEART IS LIKE A SINGING BIRD
MY HEART IS LIKE A FIGGY TREE

MY HEART IS SPLIT ASUNDER

He took me to the banquet hall.
He wrapped me in a flag of love—

Merrily

Merrily

Merrily

Each night the lascivious

marches into our wee heads

My people, les esclaves de la cuisine

who expect nothing.

My people, untouchables, who expect nothing.

≤

My people, temperate people, who expect nothing.

My people, frugal people, who expect nothing.

My people, humble people, who expect nothing.

My people, humble people, who expect nothing.

My people, gypsy people, who expect nothing.

My people, the cicada people, who expect nothing.

My people, lingering people, who expect nothing.

My people, long-lived people, who expect nothing.

My people, humble people, who expect nothing.

My people, jungle people, who expect nothing.

My people, spirit people, who expect nothing.

¥○ȲȲ ◯ é á

My people, humble people . . .

NADA-ROOO

Between Ecstasy and the Trash Can

The man did not put a rope around his neck, nor
did he shoot himself, he carried on living—

Hope is a feathered thing . . .

America provides the atmosphere

Hope is a lentil thing . . .

¥○ȲȲ   ○

with mourning and weeping
with sackcloth and lentils

In the management of her affairs
she stuck to the advice of her estate manager,
a one-eyed Ukrainian—

a cunning old rogue he used to say:
'Age be fat 'n' wise, youth be thin in size,'

winking his only eye—

with mourning and weeping
with sackcloth and lentils

Guess who's coming to dinner . . .

I HEAR THE VOICES THAT WON'T BE COOKED   *Natty Dreadlock*

II

Debra Di Blasi

Pricks: 1951

Big Bad Wolf owned the biggest car dealership in Los Angeles. Biggest Ford dealership in the country. He'd seen the father's fabulous figure and figured he'd find a way to make it work for his weekend Sale-O-Rama, sucking in all the little wifeys by making all the big hubbies feel little in the crotch and hence in life. Beta male, zeta male, theta pi omega male, all demoted and deflated by the alpha male's colossal prick demanding their attention: They could see its head a battering ram against the soft serge of his trousers.

The father no longer wore underwear, out of spite: "I'll make the whole undie industry go bust by showin' 'em panties are for girls."

He tried to think of a way to get rich from the *au naturel* look, but it was too hard thinking, too hard to make something out of nothing. So after a week he forgot about thinking and settled into the comfort of swinging free and easy.

And he was free.

And he was easy.

And that's why Big Bad Wolf dressed in wool came a-courtin'.

Knock. Knock.

"Who's there?"

"Wolf!"

"Who the hell's Wolf?"

"He's the guy who's gonna make you one rich motherfucker, that's who."

"Rich," said the father. "Now that's more like it."

The father had balls, that's for sure. And surfeit of cock. So that the stack of Jacksons should've been just a down payment on a sizeable loan. But Big Bad Wolf being what he was was so filled with envy at the sight of the father naked and proud—

hung like a horse and hands on hips happy—that he shriveled up miserable, smaller than small, to nearly nothing, and his fatuous fuck's face bled red to the cheeks and jowls, then went white. Sick he was, in skin and out, with rage against god and life and the father—*all three, trinity wrapped up in one a-fucking-mazing sausage casing*—that he closed his eyes briefly as if against a blinding bright light, and in that moment of darkness saw what he had to do, would do, could should do to the father: do: the only thing that would set the world straight and spinning right and fair: Wolf ass on a tree branch and mouthful of monkey meat.

* * * * *

In what's left of the jungle the alpha chimp kills a baby monkey and sits hunched on a high branch peeling back the skin from the bitty belly.

Yum yum!

That's what beta chimp thinks. Thinks, *I want.* Reaches out his hairy hand. Thinks, *Gimme!* And alpha chimp looks at the outstretched hand, then at beta chimp's eyes which are averted lest his request be misconstrued as demand. Alpha rips a piece of meat from the monkey's belly. Nibbles it.

Beta grunts.

Alpha lifts high the meat. Thinks, *What'll you gimme for it?*

Beta thinks, *My balls.*

* * * * *

The father reached for the Jacksons.

"Nuh-uh," said Big Bad Wolf, snatching money away. "You gotta earn it."

So the father signed the same contract the mother'd signed a year before. Fluid indenture, expandable: addendum after addendum tacked on whenever Big Bad Wolf wanted more than the fathermother'd give. Might as well been their souls they sold for all the money they'd see from it.

But all the money they'd see *because* of it? Another story.

Well, this story later. Soon enough.

* * * * *

We arrive, then, now at the moment. Narrow the past forward, squeeze the future backwards. It all comes down to a sliver between here and there, this and that, yes and no, stop and go. How when where one comes into being.

This moment here: Big Bad Wolf punches his office intercom and, fat cigar-in-mouth, grouches, "Hey, Betty Boop My Gal Sal Friday, send in Beauty, will ya."

Sucks on his cigar. Rolls it between his shiny-spit lips. Pulls it out and looks at the smoldering head. Says to the father. "Wait'll ya see this dame. I'd fucker myself 'cept my wife'd have my nuts in a vise. Zif she didn't already. Har har dee-har!"

"Har," laughs the father, confused, until beauty walks in. Floats. Spring cloud of sweet meadow fragrance and rose petal skin and dove-flutter eyelashes all aflutter at him, fine fella, finest, she thought, she knew. She, like he, had such taste.

Mmm, I'd like to taste the skin of his neck.
Like to lick the salt from her thighs.
Give him a bushel and a peck.
Drown deep wet in her green wet eyes.

And:

The moment's come—ping!—and gone. You're indelible now, already going to be, cannot not be undone by Time's Arrow shot like the father's wad.

So you are *I am.*

Me: Lucy.

* * * * *

Luce meaning light, see?

Lucid: to see clearly.

Lucy, patron saint of eye ailments and writers and artists. Martyred virgin burned, tortured, eyes torn out, throat stabbed, neck hitched to oxen yoke.

Me, saint or virgin?

Ha ha, no no.

The father named me after Lucille Ball. *I Love Lucy,* his favorite TV show. Made him laugh, that Lucy. Lit his heart, tickled his funny bone, tripped him toward belief in goodness inside badness, the bad flaking off like dead skin revealing the creamy-pink babyass new good beneath.

"Daddy do!" he grinned at me. "Lucy love!"

"Lucy Goosey," scowled the mother. "Honk!"

* * * * *

In the beginning what I did not know fit snug inside the pockets of my little fists, so perfectly cozy I assumed that what *was* was what should *be:* The father adoring me, the mother abhorring me. Thought things fit the shape of things: every peg in its own hole, and some holes pegged and some not.

Wanted the mother's love? Sure. Needed her love? Of course. Got her love? No. Blamed her? Never.

What I know now: The mother's body betrayed her and thus she me. Hormones *spfizzling* out of control, firecracker warehouse and my father a lit match dropped, one tough motherfucking spermatozoon zooming upstream faster, further to the egg that must have looked like the reachable moon, luminescent, breakable crust, the battering ram of my father's cockseed at the door.

The mother was never awestruck with motherhood motherwonder. Rather, changes in tits and ass manifested horror: Lon Chaney in a wig under a full moon, she thought. *Grrrrrrrr-l!* Moon of her belly-me signifying only the loss of waistline, skin tone and texture, varicose veins and stretch marks creepy-crawling like worms on pavement after a downpour.

"Going to pot," she called it, standing naked in front of a full-length mirror, bursting into tears at the thought of the father fucking flat-bellied women, though he swore fidelity. Said he'd cut off the nose on his face to prove it. To which she replied, "Ick!" and bawled harder.

Not herself and growing less so. By the time she spit me out of her womb too many of the chemicals she was weren't. And it wasn't that she wouldn't love me but that she couldn't.

I can't I can't I can't! she screamed at the father offering me like a protoplasmic libation to his forever goddess.

Just try, Baby!

I'll kill myself! No!

I will!

Please, I love you!

Oh!

I watched the pretty lights between them scatter in ashen clutter around their ankles and I fell dead silent, corpse still, closing my eyes and disappearing into the teeming darkness behind my lids so I would not be the wedge of their cleaving.

Eventually the father's arms grew tired of holding me out and the mother's eyes grew tired of crying: *I'm sorry.*

Why?

Everything.

Baby.

Underspoken agreement on how it would be: me forever in the backseat of their 3-speed life.

Excerpted from the novel *Birth of Eros*, forthcoming November 2022 from KERNPUNKT Press.

DARA WIER

THREE POEMS

THINGS THAT ARE LIKE ARE NOT THE SAME

A laugh's a cut
to a scar
that's burning
a look's a blow
to a simmering pain
who was it who
made you believe
you were less
than worth
the world
who turned you
inward into self-loathing
and got away scot-free
to keep on loving

THE MOON I KNOW HAS NOT BEEN WALKED UPON

Do you walk on the moon
Who walked on the moon
Who might have walked on the moon
Why did they not walk on the moon
To walk on the moon thus far
Having just occurred that one time
Why has it not become routine
Why has no one else been invited
To walk on the moon
Many nights I commune with the moon
As though we are in a committed relationship
That's all there is, just me and the moon
The moon appears then to be my real friend
It is no sign of love to walk on a friend

Rebarbative Catastrophe & Our Orphan Orange

Dying in New York City isn't the same as dying anywhere else
Every single time the feeling is exactly the same

Is why you go back to it, addicted again
As if to be afraid of being afraid would be the same

As dying in New York City as if that
Kind of fear's cost comes steep and never ends

Dying in New York City isn't like dying anywhere else
And lamentably regret aggregates

Like small avalanches of pea-sized stones
Not yet registered on an economic indicator index

Suppose everyone else turns out to be you
As from afar is most likely the case

As from afar, *from far out in far out outer space*
Dying in New York City isn't like dying anywhere else

It is like rebar lying around waiting for something to happen
Hadn't you better stop waiting to stop as you step—

Had you better not stop long enough to spend time
With the ones you love?

Up to and even including your own self
There's never enough of you to go around

There everything you've ever known and loved
Like dying in New York City where to linger is to jam

Up the works when you die in New York City your glasses fog
but not your eyes fixed on what's coming by on the river

The illusion of time is coming like dying in New York City
Is maybe an illusion I like it when they say take away time

And they do it and finally everything is happening all at once
Like dying in New York City comes strolling along

On the river always coming out of nowhere and disappearing
Into nothingness around a bend of forever

Into what's not there they say there are over 3.7 million cubicles
In New York City many of them empty

There's a certain wind that blows through me in such as way
That it feels as if every cell in my body is crying and I wonder

Does this feel good or is it something I should not be feeling
On a morning it's raining a summer rain in the winter

In New York City it is luminescent which ought to be sufficient
And that ought to be enough

And all the while it is
it is never not

R.S. Mengert

Two Poems

What it Means

The machine in the animal is more real
than the animal, because it is
the machine in all things,

real and unreal.

It generates
the pulsation of the heart. It generates
the color red:

mouth, blood, organs,

fire. The machine is both the rock
and the ships that crash on it, the tree stump
and the tired woman

who sits on it in the ice storm

at midnight. The machine
is the clock and the time it keeps
and the metallic motion of the gears.

It generates the truth

of colors and kinesis.
It completes
the darkness.

Do not ask it what it means.

It is the story
which answers questions
without speaking.

The Accidents

I.

We have been dying under this sun for years.
Dust. All the light shows
is dust.
You can only use so much of that.
Defer your questions, even the holy ones,
to the Ancient and Fraternal Order of Accidents.
They know things. The accidents
know things we will never know.

II.

Here is the one, the now,
the empty placeholder of earth
beneath you. Here is death
stripped naked in its innocence and beauty,
glistening, golden in the dark.
Chew on that awhile, what it means
to truly be alone.
Cemeteries, hospitals, offices, anyplace
can be a waiting room.

III.

Do not listen to the noise.
It will lie to you each time. Listen
to the vision. Listen to the light:
stone, water, dust.
It speaks with silence and can never lie.
Here, we will melt into the singularity
of all moments: stone, water, dust
to which we all return.
We will melt
into the accidents which know all things.

Chase Dayton

Non Serviam

T he forces of market and the laws of physics appear to be conspiring against me and they most certainly are. The restaurant continues to increase in size in direct proportion to the demands of the party I've been elected to serve. Accordingly, my capacity to supply is diminishing at the same rate. It's clear things are only going to get worse unless I do something. It's not clear I can do anything.

And then She arrives, carried in like the Ark of the Covenant. She radiates a dreadful desire that is need itself. It suffuses the atmosphere with an ancient mood of mystery and annihilation. It's clear things are going to get exponentially worse, the double binds tighter, the symmetries more fearful, the stress unredeemable unto permanent deformation.

It's Sean Penn's grandmother's birthday party and She needs a margarita. There is nothing that could be more serious. As if the whole meaning of birthdays could unravel for all time, existence as we know it negated, humanity aborted.

This, Her need, is what compels digestion and forms galaxies. Everything matters, becomes matter, on the basis of this kind of total desire. Hers. Seeking satisfaction. This isn't a mere drink order, it's a drink imperative, the logistics of the essence of thirst on which reality depends, a physical law made potable. It is the imperative of to be or not to be. And I know I will be no longer if I do not get her a goddamn margarita. Oh how I must be, and however I must, I must, if only I am but a cog in a cosmic margarita machine. I just wish the bar was where it usually was, had always been until now!

There she sits, a graven monolith, grandmatrix of cosmic fatality. I can only see her from the corner of my eye, a corner that demands to be the frame

by haunting the picture. An eye that cannot look away. This Ishtar, this Lillith, this Plutonic Mona Lisa's lurk, becoming the ambience of my life's dependence. The projection of all the biological processes mere humans must remain normally ignorant of, of their autonomy and desire. The alienation of my own body becomes familiar.

Without question it is through Grandma's margarita-need that Mr. Penn becomes his most Saturnian, his most Dantean. What makes his vibe so Titanic. For He is the fatal agent of Her thirst's principle desire. And neither will be denied anything less than total existential satisfaction. For why else enter a Buffet to begin with? I fill with quakes, my cells rumble and clank. The endocrine system grovels, the blood scrapes and gropes against its arterial walls, the eyes plead for a different function.

Him. Oh no. Him I can see all too clearly. He is clairaudient in his unspoken directions to me, about that goddamn margarita. Like his grandmother he is a silent menace, though more immediate, active—living fucking oblivion in tailored leather—scarier than anyone. Mr. Penn is that which transforms wants into needs, wishes into commands, intention into attention. He is an imperative force of nature, a viral henchman of Need, agent of desire. A Genie from a lamp forged in the mythic elemental fires of Mount Doom. An enzyme from the Belly of the Beast.

He can and will kill me, Mr. Penn. Hahaha there is *no* mistaking his capability, my mere expendability. It is clear I simply absolutely must get this drink to her as if Mr. Penn's life depended on it, as mine certainly does. I need not ask about the margarita's specifications, nor its Pharaonic and embalming nature. I just know that she knows that I just know that it is to be frozen and salted with an extra shot of Grand Marnier and four cherries. She emanates the facts of her desire, Her infernal mood. This is the urgency of fate. This is the uncanny presence of a manifest destiny. Sean Penn is here to make sure the future has a goddamn margarita with her name on it, that what will happen will happen. I feel his eyes burrow into the back of my head and I know: five, five cherries.

Thus more guests arrive, just in time for more guests to arrive. A parade of demands, a carnival of unsettling people refusing order, ordering. I go. If I can just serve the margarita all will be ok. There is hope that I can and it will. I go. If I can. Unforeseen obstacles cast a shadow of a doubt.

The bar is not where it should be, where it has always been, and suddenly I'm in a wheelchair. Mr. Penn has incorporated my emotional state into my own body, linked my mind to my body. I'd love to hate him but I just don't have that luxury, and besides, he would know. For my own benefit I need to at least think that there is a possibility of him mistaking my fear and compliance for love and competence. So I go in quest of the bar wherever it would be, has to be, somewhere.

Instinctively, like a rat, I know I need to get outside this place in order to get oriented, to find a way back inside to where the bar, and the salted grail goblet will be. The consummation of my mystery.

Fortunately, I am able to exit, the door being where it should be. I wheel towards it, forcing a smile, a winning one I hope, out of habit, like a rat.

From the outside, the restaurant is a warehouse-shaped steamship of a building with the façade of a Reno-ish strip club palace overlooking some dusty street in the French Quarter of El Paso that is completely deserted and far, far too bright and lonely. I just know I hate it. I am wheeling, up to and around to where I must go, feeling hope, wheeling and feeling I'm making a wake through the mud of panic, feeling locomotional and the optimistic cleanse of self-propulsion, of a path made clear and taken, getting there . . .

There is where I'm as lost as ever, lost as a thud in dampness, in a thick and gross part of the restaurant I know I *shouldn't* be in. I hate every-

thing that is this, everything I'm in. Also, I don't know where the bar is from here. Nor where it is from anywhere, from wherever I am. My own perspective has lost its privilege. Everything is relative and again I'm my own grandfather.

The restaurant's operating as usual, unconcerned with my ordeal, indifferent to my existence, unchanged by my motions. Despite the fact that I am extraordinarily immersed in my own imperative, I cannot access the ordinary. The satisfaction of need is the maintenance of the ordinary, the need for anyone who has a name. It's imperative we keep it.

So I find my way back outside, from inside, to an expanded vista of unexpected contingency, tracing the arcs of rabid conspiracies, whatever that might mean. But I'm sure I now know the meaning of 'no' in its edificial aspect. And that knowing what you don't care to ever know, what isn't worth finding out, is the better part of wisdom. But there is as yet no clear way out of the infernal classroom of this sinister pedagogy and bizarrerie so I must continue to learn the hard way about the futility of knowing anything at all.

The building has grown an urgency and promises to continue to do so, the kind of thing that is obvious to any human person, the concrete resonant antipathy, windows like the dead eyes of psychopathy. The bleary sky is red with advanced mourning. The street is malevolent with secret activity, its devouring aspect is very pervasive and the stuff of grimness. I must avoid it or not even hate will mean anything anymore. Time is being taken from me with increased greed. Urgency's building. My wheels' turnings, an engine for some hope. I turn to re-enter anew.

*)

I find a way!!! Back inside, from outside. There I find that the bar is in sight. I feel a sense that I am about to be handsomely rewarded, this a test I have passed and I am about to be given the throne of the Grail King, the foolish servant given the World. I think yes yes yes this will pass into something that will be called destined glory, the past but a necessary ordeal. I am reliving all of history. Until, again, I am undone by my own fantasies, my past, my obsessions, my negative capability and positive incapacitation . . .

Alas. Worse now. Than I could've seen at the time . . .

I see that Sean Penn sees me, the nightmare to end all sleep, that is. He feels something like murderous, feeling how he looks. Looks that make things clear, that observe for me the actual into existence. He is in actuality the ordinary I have fled from.

I see that I am a worthless worm-man and deserve oblivion, but only after eternal suffering, Mr. Penn salting the rim of the drain he is going to shove me down with his big black boot. And my, God, those Boots. His gaze directs me back to the party. I realize I am now crawling. He dictates my mode of getting where he needs me to be. His capacity is my incapacity. Back at the party, a new wave of the bad old feeling crashing into the old new feeling more vague as it becomes my feeling of being alive. I am drowning.

In my fixation on Grandma's need I have again missed the larger picture. I have missed the need for the margarita, the restaurant for the bar. This lack of systemic awareness is my fatal and fundamental defect for which I will be destroyed, why I have found myself being decontextualized by Mr. Penn's Carpathian gaze. I have been negligent of others. Yes, every voyage of self-discovery eventually founders on the rocks . . . Frozen and salted . . . oh no oh no :

More guests have arrived and are biting their lips, shaking the ice in their empty glasses in the rhythmic unison of the kind of tribal judgment that precedes a sacrifice. I must not do nothing. But I can do barely anything. My God, those boots. I crawl towards the arriving guests with as much enthusiasm and capability and humility and joy that I can gather so that Mr. Penn can observe my efforts and forgive my defects. But the bar is not in sight. I tell myself nothing. My thoughts have never been so flaccid. Maybe I've given up hope. Or maybe hope just stopped needing to be. I force a smile and slowly crab walk towards the crowd of awful clatter, smiling wildly.

Through the thunder of the crowd I hear the voice of the Grandmatrix speak to me through the voice of Mr. Penn, her mercenary ventriloquist —

This isn't what we ordered! And besides, we asked for more of it! And another diet coke for our children and their children and every child, may they eat free forever after. Bring us wine for our mothers and good prices for our fathers and clean doggie bags for our cats. May bread save us all in proportion to our hunger. Know: we will not be denied our worth in steak sauce! Bow your head and worship our allergies, lay prostrate before our perceived intolerances. Cheer our selections and affirm our place in the world of fad diets. Hallow our occasions, for they are the meaning of your life. Know that we are always correct and you are nothing but what confirms what we know. We demand you repeat your specials until they turn to mush in your mouth. Humor our interrogations and foibles and laugh appropriately but leave us alone already! But not for too long. We demand the justice of total attention to our needs. Bring us your manager's manager's manager. For we have changed our minds, we forgot to say. More are arriving and will continue to arrive. And we're over here, just way over there, and we may decide to move tables again. And it will be all separate checks and have you been saved by Jesus Christ? Here, take this in lieu of a tip, your salvation is far more important than money. Just know we are on our lunch breaks so hurry. Are you not writing any of this down?

Then I realize I do not have a pen. How could I possibly satisfy from memory alone?! And then Mr. Penn pulls a pen from his pocket and clicks it and clicks it and clicks it and clicks its and

Evening Thoughts

I

Nosebleeds set the boundaries of childhood.
I sought pointless strain to prove my import,
brashly subdued any bookish remnants.
Yet sunlight's brazen caress persisted.

I was born an infirm mess, the rag doll
of dainty happenings and trivial talk.
How could I not hold in awe the brutish,
that which lays claim to vexatious portions?

I kept my unsound body an adherent—
impaired lungs, flat feet, and fickle skin
begrudged the faith, and blood cascaded.
Weakness has its ways to feign ignorance.

The wished-for savagery came in ailments,
in nights of trenchant imploration and fear,
in nights tailored to instigate memory.
No protracted rigor could surge from dearth.

To be sure, false vitality quickens
through an elfin channel toward oceans
of negligible insights and hard-won dread.

II

It is the moment of guessing,
the first reductionist venture.

A truss of widening desires
withers into a single bloom—
outside bent's outcome.

What to do with this bequest
passing as a deep verity?

Care is taken to conserve
the arrant adventitious—
a now mute fragment.

It is the maturing of nescience,
the comfortable refusal.

And I see the days sprout abstract,
contours I need not replenish,
knowing as I know the likely.

What to do when one unlearns
amid the hardened labors?

I arrive nowhere with loss,
respectful only of vague signs
that seem to tell a story.

III

The French press sits.
I stare through the window.
Though the scene is empty,
the eloquent self-indulgence
of infants travels from afar.
I serve two cups of coffee.
The merciful aroma hovers.
I cannot understand
the associations;
they are mild,
dull at times.
But they hold together
the damning portrait,
don't they?
A day in bed,
a dubious joke,
routine chatter,
lukewarm meals.
All flat. All quite forgiving.
I inhale and I remember.

At Shore

Have you not suspected imprisonment
in the faithfulness to the canons of coherence,
bindings of the soul to habitual image—
forced monotone of meanings and sudden compromise?

I take the sky in wonder—
now as current under tenuous nets,
now as confluence of nerves,
now as self-regulating gothic.

Have you not seen the dunes that gather at dawn,
sculpted into dissolution through thriving geometries?
Ignored errantry, as ephemeral
as it is compact—creation in prodigal seconds.

I reach for the sea that lurks
beneath the tiles and seize a stem's sap.
In the dateless tide of each,
everything stands for everything else.

Resolution

I will long for the hopelessly concrete,
for the nurture of presence, only tie
to a waning body—in time renounced.

The temptation of exodus
lingers and tests my patience.

I choose the warmth of familiar outlooks.
Is not closeness to novelty a kind
of death, a stifling of natural growth?

I will yield to daydreams and yearnings
when the roots turn into wires.

Alan McCormick

If the Head Had It

V

If the head had ever had it, now it had gone. Shaping west, making out with anything that comes its way, scrambled Fray Bentos aerial, dog food brain. Made my money in cool Velcro pants that'd hug a greyhound tight, chased rabbits round and round, back to front, y oh why am I so shy? See him then, dwarf's cap, a tight mince-pimp-walk like he's just secreted a foil capsule up his choke and is squeezing his cheeks to keep it from falling; one eye out for the bluebottles, one eye out for a score.

'Please, I'm all at sea, I need to land!'

'Go, fetch!' and he chucks it over the churchyard wall.

Over I follow, scrabbling by a gravestone and digging around the dead, my mind about to spurt.

Father Derek appears. He senses my urgency: 'God has plans for you, Michael. God has plans for me. God has plans for everyone.'

'A planner, this God, is he?'

'He is.'

'That's it?'

'It is.'

I see it poking from under his shoe.

'God bless you, Father.'

Up the steps to the steeple I go, knees to elbows, lungs emptying, heart poking through the chest bone, horizons all merging at the top. Sweet unwrap; sour musk tongue, head expanding—botulism from an arse's arse, my hands join in prayer, a diver's poise, ground swelling up and body going down.

'Some come here and jump like Eddie the Eagle, making spectacles of themselves,' is all Father Derek will say.

'Eddie the Eagle wore glasses,' I might reply if I were still able to. Poor calculation for a jumper though: Eddie never reached enough speed for lift off and his bulk always dragged him down.

'God has plans for you,' Father Derek had said.

And that made no sense at all.

Passing over the rooftops, pink-grey grime of ridged Toblerone, chimneystacks belching out reclaimed pallet fumes. Mum's house sits silent, a fog of doom, her black cloud engulfing the kitchen, Guinness pinafore bustling, the toucan cast out of paradise to crumple at her lap as she gets to polishing, casting out demons: her son, a jumper, a bailer out:

'There's a priest, a rabbi, an imam and a junkie standing together in a hot air balloon. The balloon is falling to the ground. One has to agree to jump to save the others. The religious men start praying.

"I'll get my needle," says the junkie.

"No!" the religious men shout but too late, no calculation needed and the balloon plummets to the ground.'

The whistle on the kettle screeches. Father Derek arrives to offer prayer, his dark figure looming on the glass panel of the front door, and Mum screams as if she's seen a ghost.

*

The first time was with Katherine, artistic bohemian Katherine from the other side. Her father was an architect, her mother an art teacher, fragrant stock to a lowlife like me. A newbie at university studying maths, a geek in every sense from my home-knit Feargal Sharkey cardigans to my market-stall trainers, I was ripe for sabotage. Katherine wore cool black polo necks, smoked white filtered Kents and blew out circles above my head to tighten the noose, to rein me in. When she unfolded a pair of black silk pants from her bag, a syringe rolled out onto the mattress between us. She'd spotted the flaw, smelled desperation through the cracks, and knew there'd be no hesitation.

The funeral is underway and my brother Aiden is stalling: 'Michael, Michael, what can you say about Michael?'

Father Derek shrugs his shoulders as if to say 'don't expect me to answer that!' Aiden is struggling because in common with practically every one else in this sorry congregation, he hasn't seen me in years. Not only that but he'd never forgiven me for plaguing Mum when things had got rough, borrowing and stealing from her to pay a debt, to keep alive on the streets, to keep things going. Hypocrite that he is, with his fine infidelity suit, the serial womaniser with the brood safely tucked in at home, flaunting his pitiful giblet to any woman he could pass muster with.

'Michael was a beautiful young boy, who was good at maths but sadly lost his way, God rest his soul. May he find peace and salvation for his sins.'

Is that it? Is that the best he can do? The mood overall is tense rather than sad. There is some general sobbing and more and more chair scraping. People want out. Mum looks like a cadaver, the flinty cheekbones protruding under her eyes arched like chicken wings, her irises exploding bloodshot from tiny strained vessels into the white of her eyes. She looks like a junkie too now.

*

Mum in the cold clasp drape of her bed, eyes up to the cross. I blow low notes through the tiny hairs in the bassoon of her ear and she responds with a faint smile and sighs.

'Is that you?' she asks, and tries to sleep in case she finds me there.

I think of smothering, an act of kindness, but no, I fill her glass by the bed for her to put her dentures. They drop in with a fixed grin and small bubbles chase up to the rim. I kiss her on the cheek, and her eyes close.

In her sleep I am washed clean, and she is rocking me on her knees. Numbers silenced in my head for a moment, I cling on and try not to fall.

IV

1975, the year of being born, and me not yet fourteen, in a pair of coach seats to my own, near the back away from the dark lords and dusky maidens upfront—the brothers and nuns—and two up from the VIP sofa rear, the cool kids, their piss awful laughs and catcalling. An away-day escape to the jaunty seaside, mixing up hormones, tangling barbed wire braces, gum, stutter and smarting cheeks with the local convent girls.

Aiden is back there with tarty Frances, fingering away under her satchel, discreetly poised over her ugly lampshade gingham skirt. She's at it too and he makes a low moan when he comes—then a handy tissue bound in gents fluid *tossed* (!) towards the back of Kevin Connor's head, miraculously fixing onto his trailing locks—and Aiden tells me later that Frances holds onto his prick like no other. I think of a girl's fingers squeezing around a racing handlebar and get a slightly sick feeling deep inside the holy pit.

'Are you children behaving?' shouts a Brother, too lazy or too frightened to venture to the back.

'All Hunky Dory,' yells a boy with a rebel-tinge of henna to his spike-top.

'No sticky fingers round here, Bro,' says Aiden softly enough, so only Frances and his friends hear.

The hyena giggles start quiet at first, then pump up to bursting, but before madness breaks out and revolution hits the air, they artfully puncture things, hiss it all out, hot and wild eyed, gasping like they've stepped out of a furnace. Frances lets go a stunted scream, finally faking her arrival: 'took your time, Aiden,' she says, punching him on the arm, then re-arranging her skirt into an innocent pose, satchel returned to the floor by her feet.

I recite multiplication tables in my head, temples numbing out the deluge of unwanted sounds, numbers way beyond the yellowed sweaty school texts: 22x24 is 528, 23x24 is 552, 24x 24 is 576, yes, oh, fucking yes!!!

From the top of the town, the sea arrives onto the coach window, framed beside the hairy-man driver, a carpet of cool, a flagrant call to undress; I hope we don't get to see his gorilla arse and wild garden back parting the waves.

We straggle onto the pebbly beach, each group finding a rock to collect behind, to undress, fleeting hands sneaking modesty towels ('too small, Ma, I told you it was too small') away from skinny blue-white chicken flesh:

'Do that that to me again you feck, and I'll skin you of all your skin!

'That makes no fucking sense, Jon, and you know it.'

'Shit off or I'll shit on you!'

'That's better, but you've a way to go before anyone could call you a poet.'

I find a rock of my own and start counting down numbers in elevens until it's time to go: 233,000, 232,989, 232,978, all the while not being able to keep my eyes off the sea, its swirl, rise and fall; the grating shingle pull back, the letting go; patterns forming further out, globs and gloops, bubbles popping onto the surface; the draw under.

Soon enough the weakening sun rots amongst a mass of grey sweltering clouds. We congregate under a tin roof shelter, assemble for foul smelling sandwiches, fish paste as pink as Angel Delight. The milk is sour as sick but we drink it anyway. The Brothers look troubled in their inappropriate thick clothes, like bachelor herdsman driven out for the yearly pull, practising lines on each other; nuns huddled up too close in the cramped shelter, agitating towards the saviour tea flask for another sup.

'You look nice in that horsehair vest, David,'

'Thank you, Tom, you look very nice too, a grey tank-top suits you. And isn't it nice weather we've been having, Sister Anne?'

Blood violates her cheeks, a faint animal sound emitted through dry untouched lips; it may be a response or a cry for help.

Sister Bernadette steps into the breech: 'And isn't tea always welcome on a day like this.'

A murmur of approval, an away-day Amen.

*

At the end of the pier is a concrete tower, a small derelict lighthouse. It's fenced off by barbed wire, with a large sign saying 'DANGER, DO NOT EN-TER', and some nut job has scrawled in red-blood-ink under: *Enter and you will surely die. Sui-ciders welcome.*

A group of lads, Aiden, naturally, now disen-tangled from Frances's grip, have left the watch-ful eyes of the Brothers and made their way through a gap in the fence and gone inside. I fol-low up damp winding stairs. We meet on a small metal balcony at the top. A flimsy rusty railing holds us from the sea, circling way down below.

'Jesus, Aiden, Mad Michael has followed us.'

'Piss off, Michael,' says Aiden.

I stare through them, eyes to the horizon

'Mental boy, you're not wanted,' says one of the others, pushing me in the chest.

'Leave him alone,' says Aiden.

They let me be, and start discussing what order they should jump in. Pat, the one who called me Mad Michael, says he'll go first. Obviously they all want to go first but after a while they agree and he gets himself ready, the railing trembling as he climbs onto it. He tries to compose himself at the edge, taking in deep breaths, his body teetering,

arching forward, the sea looming below. He's like that for at least a minute.

'Go on, Pat, get on with it, for fuck's sake!'

'I am, I am, just don't rush me.'

'Ha ha, his legs are shaking.'

'Like Elvis, whoa, whoa.'

'Shut up, will you!'

'Jump then, you faggot.'

The boys form a chorus: 'jump! Jump! Jump!'

'I can't, I can't!'

'You're a frozen bloody chicken, Pat,' says Aiden. 'Get down'.'

Pat climbs down and Aiden takes his place.

'Jump! Jump! Jump!'

'Fuck this, lads,' says Aiden after a few mo-ments swaying at the railing.

Another boy tries. Same thing.

As he gets down, I jump up onto the railing, glance down at the sea, and go. All speeded up. The rush as I drop, breaths emptied out, my heart so heavy, it's like it's slipped down my chest and into my legs, and then a smack as I hit the surface of the water, a sheet of metal, which jars my body, re-aligning things so I can break through. I feel my left leg ripped sideways as if a Great White has grabbed it.I go under.

III

Big as the house he set himself against, Dad's bullish shoulders heaving down, the hammer striking the wall. Dust, plumes of brick ash, a one-man demolition, and the wall came crashing down. If he whacked you, you were winded for hours, flesh smarted and glowing, a bruise spreading under the skin, a sulphurous flower opening out, poisoning the bloodstream, his anger spreading through you.

Six weeks before the seaside sortie, and Mum is pushing me towards the bed in the far corner of the ward, the scent of decay and old man piss flooding the nostrils, Dad's death trolley waiting to take him away. Only Dad is 52. Shrunken, corpse-like apart from the sorry groan to greet me, an outstretched arm, emaciated and gleaming with sweat, his anchor tattoo shrivelled in the creases of his skin.

'Don't smoke, son,' he says. 'It'll rip you.' He pinches my hand, an echo of his force reduced into something singular and unmanly. He winces and points to the drip by the bed.'Hit the button, please,' he says, a formal curtsey I'd never heard him use before. And he says it again: 'Please, son. Please!'

I do as he asks and the morphine plops down the line and into his vein.

'More, he says. 'But don't let Nurse Ratched see.'

Mum arrives with a carrier bag and sits by his bed. 'I've bought some rhubarb and some apples.'

'For the love of God, woman, I don't want it. None of it.'

I hit the button and after a moment he sighs and relaxes back into the pillows, his face beatific and wan, the trace of a smile.

'It's an air bed,' Mum says. 'It's just as well he can't smoke anymore.'

Three weeks later he was gone. Ashed. Dusted away.

*

After the dive, I was rescued by a fishing boat, heaved in unconscious. When I woke in hospital, the pain was ballistic but I knew a cure. The drip was attached and screams abated, all those sums, numbers melting away. A pale mist descending onto my eyelids, an icy rush into the vein, a moment of nausea I'd come to know well, learn to push through, and then this new delicious feeling, a cossetted weight in and around me, cocooned, released from harm and responsibility.

The ward radio is on. 'Thank you for the music, for giving it to me'.

'Abba, I should hate Abba, but fuck it, they're lovely. Clean and modern, booted out in whites and turtlenecks like they're living the Space Age: lovely.'

'They often talk like this on the drip,' a nurse tells Mum.

'Will he be okay?' Mum asks, the bag of old rhubarb and apples by her feet.

'Fuck, yeah,' I say.

'Michael, don't you dare speak like that. Not even when you're ill.'

My leg is cast as Tutankhamen, mummified and snow white. Soon Aiden comes in and draws a cock and balls and his idea of a vagina, hormonal witless hieroglyphics, and I'll write the names Frida and Benny in unfamiliar girlie bubble writing beside. But mostly I sleep, and pretend to be asleep when Aiden and Mum are around, sink into the mattress, slip slowly under, swim down the depths, thrilling underwater lagoons, pearl roof caves, coral cathedrals, find sanctuary with a Terry Wogan priest in an aqualung, who makes the sign of a cross with a finger through the water.

'*Waterloo*: a famous battle between the English and the French? Or *water loo*, a form of improvised sea toilet—you can tell they're releasing when they suddenly stand still, eyes to the horizon and pretend they're thinking something profound—or the name of a song written for Eurovision by the popular Swedish pop group, Abba?'

'Would I be right in saying it's the name of a song written for Eurovision by the lovely Swedish pop group, Abba?'

'Lovely is right, Mad Michael, you have won—'

'Push the buzzer, Terry.'

And before the nurse comes running, another dose, precise and perfect, is released.

Lovely. Just lovely.

II

Once Katherine glowed, 'a gift to the dark' people used to say. After years on the street, any glow had dimmed. Best viewed in shadow, stressed and skeletal, ravaged like a street cat, missing teeth, clumps of hair ripped out, eyes blazing and approaching any man in the street that has a pulse.

'Five for a blow job!'

'I'm not going to give you a blow job.'

'What? No, don't be funny, please. Come on, my arse could be yours for ten, do anything for as long as you like.'

'You don't have an arse, you skinny bitch.'

If he carried on, I'd step out of a doorway and give him a slap: 'run, student boy or the ghost of her teeth will chase you around town and bite off your cock!'

'My knight in shining armour but you should just fuck off, he would have given in.'

'Nah, don't think so, Kat, you were barking up the wrong tree there.'

'Woof, fucking woof!'

'Come on, we can share.'

'You won't want me to do anything?'

'Damn right, but some peace and quiet would be nice.'

We kissed, her mouth sucking me in, but if I closed my eyes her lips felt full again, tongue tipping, lightly touching where once were teeth, that tingle through my body again.

We shared a squat, damp as a paddy field, the acid smell of vomit, always losing our sleeping bags so eventually we didn't bother. I came down with pneumonia so badly that I ended up in hospital, and when I was kicked out after two weeks, Katherine was gone.

Rumour on the street was that her parents had mounted a rescue. I always thought she'd come back, but as years passed, no sight or sound. Then, one day, I saw her across the road, kitted out like a de-mobbed nun on her first weekend away, shapeless in a flowery skirt and frilly blouse, an auntie's wig up top, and a set of dentures that would grace a small horse.

'Kat,' I shouted but she didn't so much as look up.

For good measure, an elderly couple—the retired architect and art teacher I'm guessing—caught up with her and pulled her along.

A few days later she came and begged me to help her get away.

We scored just like the old days but I hadn't taken into account how clean she'd become. A miscalculation, and it took her away for good, eyes up to the night sky, filling with dark; the needle traces, apart from the latest, magically disappeared in the snow of her arms, her gleaming white falsies meeting in a fabulous unintentional grin.

I

After she went and died, I took up bothering Father Derek. Not the most patient of men, easily given to cliché, but at least he tried.

'God has plans for you!' he said.

I really should have asked what he meant. And a better man than me might have jumped but I actually tripped and fell. Statistics could have taken that into account and helped lessen the load.

Lying on Mum's lap, the numbers in my head re-surface, start to count me down, 5-4-3-2-1, and I want to shout out 'Thunderbirds' but I'm already gone.

Selin Tamtekin

Today's Dreams are Tomorrow's News

When I went to Istanbul last March and visited Murat Yıldız at his studio—straight after untimely heavy snowfall had covered the city in white—I found him preparing for his first solo exhibition, currently ongoing at Öktem Aykut.

A succession of bomb attacks that took place in Turkey in 2015 triggered an awareness in Yıldız, which, having centered his production around it, he continues to explore through various art experiments: how people and objects shape one another.

For instance, with his recorder at hand, Yıldız walks for hours across various Turkish cities, recording, as he goes along, every word and sentence he hears. Subsequently, he transcribes them to create non-narrative books made up of words and sentences that are independent of one other.

With this exercise the artist aims to looks at how he is unconsciously shaped by others. He explains:

"When I'm on the street, I keep hearing things and they are most probably, one way or another, unconsciously shaping me. I feel differently if I see people fighting, compared to how I feel when I come across those who are uttering love words or are talking calmly to each other."

Yıldız is always in deep thought—with a demeanor which suggests he's hardly ever able to disengage from his pursuit of solving life's puzzle. The intensity in his eyes reflects the turbulence he seems to be harboring behind a calm exterior.

While referring to a memory from his childhood spent in Balâ (a village near the capital Ankara) around the ages of five or six, it becomes evident that even then his mind was preoccupied with existential reckonings:

"I would run but it led me nowhere because Ankara is very flat and bare. This taught me that no matter how hard I run I will get nowhere."

After offering me some coffee, Yıldız proposes, "Come, be my eye, if you like," and I accept.

We walk next to a large work on the wall, concealed behind a piece of drapery covering the work from end to end. The instant the artist begins to remove it he immediately shuts his eyes, while abstract gestures made with pencils, pastels, markers and ink on a broad white sheet of paper appear.

The unframed work belongs to his 'Non-Eye Centric Drawings' series where, by following instructions given to him by others, the artist looks at how people are able to consciously shape him.

For a while, from where I stand, I carefully examine the relationship between the different interventions previously made on the paper.

"There are two parallel lines running horizontally across the picture. You could draw something in a neutral color to reduce their overbearing presence," I suggest.

Continuing to keep his eyes closed, he asks me to choose paint from a paintbox nearby. After I decide on a grey pastel, I hand this over to Yıldız and he quietly places it in his pocket.

On the picture plane, I direct his hand to where I wish him to make his mark. Since he will administer this once I have left, in order to keep the spot in his mind, he quickly measures in hand-spans how far it is to the corners of the paper—with the dexterity of someone who has adapted himself to moving without seeing. After that, he covers the drawing and finally opens his eyes.

At first glance, these colorful drawings can evoke the subjectivity of abstract expressionism and its individual effort to create something original. Everyone and everything in the universe are a part of a gigantic web of relations where they 'shape' and are 'shaped.' While creating, artists are continuously stimulated by people, objects and other entities within their mental and physical radars. Thus, every work of art carries an autobiographical element and when evaluated in this context, 'originality' becomes a highly debatable concept.

"Who am I? In fact, I'm the neighborhood I presently live in. It determines how I behave, and I influence how it appears. Nothing is independent of anything else, everything affects everything else," Yıldız stresses at one point in our conversation.

The artist, who sets no boundaries in assessing how people can consciously shape him, sometimes encourages visitors to spontaneously draw on the paper or canvas, thereby allowing them to contribute directly to his art production—as if to further defy the notion of authorship.

Moreover Yıldız points out that since it's his partner of many years, artist Defne Tesal, who is most frequently nearby, it is predominantly she who decides on each work's dimensions, when they are deemed complete and ultimately how these drawings will appear aesthetically.

Depending on the simplicity and intensity of their compositions, they reflect a poetic sensibility or with disparate marks overlapping and transforming into scribble, a rebellious kind of exuberance.

Of these drawings which are the product of a collective effort Yıldız says:

"I like the fact that everything is fusing and deriving from itself. On the other hand, it's chaos . . . Am I creating my own chaos through others?" he asks himself, pondering for a moment.

Two works included in the show, which are stylistically at polar opposites with this series, are in fact, in terms of content, directly connected with it. One is "Defne's Eye", where the artist has depicted Tesal's eye.

"The eye is my eye, in other words it's Defne's eye. I wanted it to represent all the other eyes that have shaped this exhibition," reflects Yıldız.

The other piece is the self-portrait of the artist with his eyes shut.

When I come across this drawing at Yıldız's studio it's at the stage of near completion. While carefully examining it up close, for a moment I'm captivated by the textural softness—depicting every fine detail, including each hair strand, with light retouches—the artist has been able to capture and by the tenderness the work possesses.

"In the picture, I have five sweaters on because I had to wear five layers all winter while I was here," Yıldız complains.

His ground floor studio, despite a small electric heater in one corner, is still too cold for me to even attempt taking my coat off.

Yıldız points to a few different-sized spheres on the ground—still in the making. He explains that after gluing forty to fifty newspapers together and painting them over, he sands them down to achieve a smooth surface.

"In order to stay warm, I've been sanding them down from dawn to dusk," he remarks with a soft smile.

These 'Satellites' currently being exhibited at Öktem Aykut take the notion of how every entity in life's ever-changing cycle is 'shaped' and 'shapes' into a cosmic dimension.

Yıldız remarks: "Satellites circle around planets and appear to be under their influence but actually a planet is also an orbit's orbiter. I perceive satellites as things that orbit around and affect me, but at the same time, at any moment I can also become the other's satellite."

At the beginning of this June, Yıldız and Tesal traveled to Mardin—a city in the Eastern part of Turkey. There they visited Kamer Foundation, a center for counseling and support for women who have experienced severe trauma due to violence, discrimination or sexual abuse. There, for four days, the artists encouraged refugees and asylum-seekers from different ethnicities to write down and illustrate their dreams.

While at his studio, Yıldız tells me how, with time, his curiosity for 'the way people and objects shape one another' evolved into questions that have paved the way to other art experiments. One of these is, 'Can people shape their own future?'

Taking this question as a starting point, through an art initiative they have been carrying out since 2019, Yıldız and Tesal visit various institutions and initiatives and offer people there to write down and illustrate their dreams in a big, blank notebook they have prepared in the format of a newspaper. Then they print and distribute this handwritten newspaper embellished with words and drawings full of hope.

Before I leave his studio, skeptical of whether such an exercise could make any difference, I lastly pose the question, "Can people really shape their future with their dreams?"

After thinking for a while, the artist answers with conviction, "Today's dreams should be tomorrow's news—for we have no other choice," as if to emphasize the importance of never giving up hope, no matter what.

This article was first published in Turkish on the website of T24 in June 23, 2022.

Murat Yıldız's solo exhibition *Water is a Sandpaper, You Are My Eye* was on display at Öktem Aykut, Istanbul (https://oktemaykut.com) from May 28 to 2 July 2022.

MARK DUCHARME

It

I didn't watch it, or I tried not to anyway.
I don't own a watch on Sundays.
I sleep, some of the time.
I am always where I am when I said you were.
If I were you, I wouldn't know
Whom to be.
If I were myself, where should I lie?
Are you me now, in passing?
Do I own some of the clouds that rise
When the wind is full of stars?
Is there any other day that seems to be?
Who is it, just another mirage?
The past is truth, & youth fades
Always, in cold company
Withheld, in modern panic.
& Now, you're going back
Until when? If I haven't yet damaged
The light on this field trip for elective frailty
Will your cold dark eyes still know
The shadow I become?

"The Pen She Guides Doesn't Translate"

HIST
James Belflower and Matthew Klane
Calamari Archive, Ink., Sept. 2022

In the introduction to Belflower and Klane's graphic novel, *HIST*, the authors talk about making a pilgrimage to a town whose name is derived from its "favorite son." My initial thought was Cooperstown, an incredibly beautiful small town located on a lake not far from where I live. It's named after its founder William Cooper, whose son is celebrated author James Fenimore Cooper of *Leatherstocking Tales / Last of the Mohicans* fame. But I almost immediately doubted myself; not everything is centered around my life. Besides, there was no mention of baseball anywhere to be found.

A little internet research surfaced that both authors are from Albany, which, in turn, made me think that the "Author" in question might be Melville. However, as I kept reading, there were hints—"Natty" and "Mr. Pump"—that affirmed I was correct in seeing Cooperstown right away. Belflower and Klane claimed to have found a book called *HIST* in a book barn during this pilgrimage, a book that contained "essentially all of the Author's data" or, in other words, a collection of Cooper's works. They claim to use this source material in the material experiment before the reader, "compressing the vastness of this literary spectrum" and running its illustrations "through a program of ritual filters, random params, and blended audio visualizers" in an attempt to capture the "textures of American literature."

I don't know if you've read Cooper, but it takes some tenacity to power through it (in my opinion). I haven't read all of the stories referenced in these pages but I don't think you need to know anything about Cooper or his work to appreciate this book. It is a beautiful transmutation of a history and familiar-even-if-not-known mythology. I'm unsure what technique the authors used: erasure, a type of cento, or if the whole premise of the original *HIST* book barn find is some postmodern invention. Regardless, the end result is a poignant and engaging retelling and, in the act of retelling, with both image and text, the authors have created something wholly new. Visually, it is a psychedelic comic book with images abstracted and patterned with color. They are really quite breathtaking and modern, even though you can make out the unmistakable firm hand of the original, antique illustrations. The authors utilize a handful of repeated images edited and manipulated to show the myriad ways there is to read that image, that text. Even with all of the vibrance and intricate patterning, some of my favorite images were where the panels looked like aged or eroded material that you might find in an old barn. One in particular, on page 45, is a simple line edged with shadow, made with shades of grey, black, and green, that reads to me like Otsego Lake on a misty day.

There are eight distinct sections or 'chapters' comprising of one 'poem' each. They are self-contained stories and the authors are adept at imbuing both tension and emotion with only sparse text. Aided by the images, the words are lyrical, affecting, and create whole worlds on a single page. Gems of the collection include: "Natty A Lover", "Birch In His Cottage", and "Narra-Mattah". Implicit in these tales, both the inspiration and the artwork, are stories of survival, lust, love, as well as racial, religious, and gendered tension. The interplay of art with text brings to light the dissonance and complexity of these stories that were once presented as black and white. Moreover, *HIST* illustrates how we can distort and alter the pattern history leaves behind. We can't abandon the past; the "American Author" is a part of our common heritage. But we can move it around to explore all of its angles, beautiful and profane.

Yeah, What the Hell Did Larry Rivers Do, Anyway?

What Did I Do? The Unauthorized Autobiography of Larry Rivers
Harper Collins, 1992

A few years back, as I was rooting through the dusty old books at the Westbeth flea market, I came across a copy of *What Did I Do? The Unauthorized Autobiography of Larry Rivers* (Harper Collins). Rivers is of course a former Chelsea Hotel resident, and his Dutch Masters Cigar Box painting, "The Presidents", which hung in the hotel lobby during the Stanley Bard years, had always been one of my favorites. The fact that the book was co-written by Arnold Weinstein, another Chelsea resident, and one with whom I had the pleasure of actually being acquainted (Weinstein died in 2005), was a further attraction. The book has a dedication: "for Mac— Christmas 92 with love from David + Susan". Now, while I have no idea who these people are, since the Westbeth building on Washington Street in the far West Village is an "artists' colony" similar to what the Chelsea used to be (although with a helpful stamp of government approval in their case), it's fun to speculate. The vast, labyrinthine basement of the Westbeth must be filled with ancient, art-related artifacts such as this book, just waiting to be unearthed. Best flea market in town.

For those of you who don't know, the Chelsea Hotel, where I've lived for the past twenty-seven years, and which had been closed for renovations since 2011, recently started renting out a few rooms on the upper floors earlier this year, also reopening the El Quijote restaurant on the ground floor. While *What Did I Do?* was published way back in 1992, I figured that, at this transitional time in the history of the Chelsea, we might take a moment to revisit our rich heritage, in order to take stock of what we've lost and perhaps even generate some ideas as to how we might best move into the future.

In any event, the book features some pretty good writing, and, while it lags in places and is over long, it's mostly exciting and engaging, especially to anybody with an interest in the New York art scene. The only real problem is that it's all over the place, such that, one moment you'll be reading about the jazz clubs on 52nd St. and the next you're flashing back to Larry's problem with pimples in high school; or one moment you're in an art gallery in the nineteen-sixties and then suddenly you're on the beach in the fifties. Apparently the intention is to create a kind of "collage", such as Rivers employed in his visual work, or maybe even an "improvisation", as he was also a jazz musician (and heavily influenced by the Beats as well, often playing his baritone saxophone as poets read aloud in Village coffeehouses). Sometimes it works, but at other times the transitions are jarring, to say the least. We could always blame Weinstein for this, but Rivers—perhaps betraying a bit of insecurity in wanting to be considered a great writer in addition to a great artist and jazz musician—takes credit for the actual writing of the book, relegating Arnold to the role of transcribing to a computer as he, Rivers, reads aloud from a series of notes while the two men sit drinking in a barn in Southampton.

As for what's good about the book, well, it has a grand sweep. Rivers knew everyone, went everywhere, and did everything—at least in the world of New York Bohemia. The entire Twentieth century is his canvas, and he makes the most of it. From a childhood in the depression and service in World War II, he goes on to study jazz at Julliard with fellow student Miles Davis, and art at Hans Hoffmann's school in Greenwich Village. He parties with Frank O'Hara and the New York School poets in the Hamptons, and stars with fellow Chelsea Hotel alumni Allen Ginsberg, Jack Kerouac, and Gregory Corso in the underground film, "Pull My Daisy". He acts in plays for the Living Theater (run by Chelsea Hotel residents Julian Beck and Judith Malina), and gets ripped off in a heroin deal by none other than the great saxophonist Gerry Mulligan. Rivers never seems to have been too political, though he does his part in the cold war by traveling to the Soviet Union to show paintings of black and white cocks ("America's No. 1 Problem") and Japanese cunts dripping with cum to the disapproving Russian artists, and though his life intersected at one point with Abbie Hoffman (yet another former Chelsea Hotel resident), who, after his (Abbie's) play at the Cherry Hill Theater, locked Larry and the rest of the audience in the theater for an hour to make a point about the Holocaust (precise point not specified). These guys weren't afraid of giving offense.

Besides all that, the book contains plenty of great illustrations: dozens of black and white photos sprinkled throughout the text, together with two sections of color plates featuring reproductions of Rivers' paintings. It's a quality book—$30 for the hardback in 1992—as Rivers clearly made sure his art was displayed to its best effect. Too bad it doesn't have an index, as, especially given the non-chronological nature of the text, it makes it difficult for the reviewer to locate specific passages, and equally hard for the casual reader to skip to the stories of their favorite stars (of which there are no shortage).

All of which brings us to the art itself. And if, perhaps, Rivers is not quite among the first rank of American artists, and his art is not as highly esteemed as perhaps it should be, many critics seem to feel, and Larry tends to believe as much himself, that it's because he's neither fish nor fowl, caught in the netherworld between competing schools of art. He employs the broad brush techniques of expressionism, but he's a figurative painter—which could definitely get you punched in the nose by Jackson Pollock or Franz Kline. And while he's sometimes called the "Godfather of Pop Art" because he often references pop cultural icons, he doesn't employ the clean lines of commercial art and he doesn't have quite the same ironical detachment from his subject matter (being a lot more transgressive than most of the pop artists, for one thing).

Rivers was as free-wheeling in his persona as he was in his art. While he freely mingles with the two-fisted Cedar Tavern types, he's flamboyant in his dress and his mannerisms, sprinkling affairs with men in with his even more numerous conquests among members the fairer sex. And while he assures us that gay men find him quite handsome, he doesn't quite fit in with them either. So there you have it: he's mercurial and hard to pin down. The only certainty is that Larry is a bad boy. The book contains myriad tales of his infamous, polymorphously perverse lifestyle. Starting with his forced initiation into the art of fellatio at the age of six at the hands of the neighborhood bully, through his attempt to coerce his younger sister into intercourse when he's ten, on through his kindly uncle's introduction to a simple minded girl who services all the neighborhood boys, we get all the sordid details. A lifelong sufferer from premature ejaculation, Rivers refuses to let this slow him down (ha ha!), and his Peyronie's Syndrome (which causes the penis to bend at a painful angle when erect) only makes things that much kinkier. In an apparent attempt to win the Heisman Trophy of Degeneracy, he tries to fuck both his sixteen-year old sister (maybe a different sister this time?) *and* his aged mother in law—though in both these instances he's drunk out of his mind and, not to trivialize his actions, but he may not be *entirely* serious. Rivers has nothing to hide, but sometimes we sense that he has a reputation to protect: he's a wild and crazy guy, and don't you ever forget it! He seems to get a kick out of shocking people, both in his art and his behavior. There's even a three way featuring his longtime subtenant and ghostwriter, Weinstein.

It's somewhat surprising to learn that, while Rivers was married twice (with five children), had numerous long-term relationships and countless flings with women, and considered himself primarily heterosexual, the great love of his life seems to have been the poet Frank O'Hara, about whom he rhapsodizes:

> I liked his Ivy league dirty white sneakers, he liked my hands full of paint. He was a charming madman, a whoosh of air sometimes warm and pleasant, sometimes so gusty you closed your eyes and brushed back the hair it disarranged. . . .Through a moist pair of lips like a Cupid's bow, he smoked and spoke with enthusiasm about the virtues of a thousand subjects. (p. 228)

And he was heartbroken when O'Hara died in a Long Island beach taxi accident in 1966, calling it, in the eulogy he delivers at Frank's graveside, "the beginning of tragedy" and his first experience of loss.

Rivers won early acclaim for his painting "Washington Crossing the Delaware" and for his nude portraits of his mother-in-law Berdie Berger (same one he later attempted to "seduce"), and his most famous work is his gargantuan mixed construction, "The History of the Russian Revolution: From Marx to Mayakovsky". But among Chelsea Hotel residents he's most fondly remembered for his Dutch Masters paintings, as a particularly good exemplar, apparently titled "The Presidents", hung in the lobby (to the right of the door, coming in) for decades. The thing I like about this piece is that it's so cleverly mind bending: the original Rembrandt painting "Syndics of the Drapers' Guild", turns a bunch of businessmen into fine art; then the cigar company turns art into crass commerce (elevating the businessmen into "Masters"); and finally Larry turns the commercial object, the cigar box itself, back into fine art (and now elevates the syndics into "Presidents"). It's pop art now, for sure, but it's almost like it was pop art all along. The piece is gone now, removed from the lobby with the rest of the art when the Chelsea was sold in 2011, though the really crass commercialists (in other words the developers who bought the building) weren't able to profit. The Larry Rivers estate sued, claiming that the artist had simply loaned the expensive cigar box to then manager Stanley Bard,

rather than—as legend would have it—paying his rent with it. It would have been a lot of rent, after all, as the painting has reportedly been valued at $400,000.

At one point in the book, Rivers recounts the evening that Frank O'Hara brought him to the Chelsea Hotel to meet the great "composer-critic-curmudgeon extraordinaire", Virgil Thompson, who immediately launched into a discourse about the importance of the skylight in painting:

> In Paris in the twenties, Gertie—Stein, that is—took him to the studios of Matisse, Picasso, Bonnard, et. al.; they all told him how important was the light of Paris, which could only truly be seen through the well-placed skylights of their ateliers. (p. 234)

Regrettably, Rivers seems to take the side of the present management, BD Hotels (who have blocked several skylights that previously opened onto the roof, including the central one in the widely celebrated staircase), for when Virgil asks him, "How's your skylight, Mr. Rivers?" he answers, perversely, "I keep it covered." Sorry Larry, but we'll have to go with Matisse, Picasso, and Bonnard on this one.

But Rivers must've liked something about the place, because in 1963, he and his second wife, Clarice, moved into ". . . the somewhat less cockroach-crowded room with designer chipped sinks, abrasive stucco walls, and constantly running hot and cold water . . . in beloved Stanley Bard's Chelsea Hotel." (p. 429) Rivers gives us his impression of the hotel at some length:

> . . . home of rock and roll bands and Leonard Cohen and Bob Dylan; Dylan Thomas and Thomas Wolfe; Brendan Behan, the Irish bard, singing Israeli songs with Allen Ginsberg; George Kleinsinger, composer and Animal lover, who lived with snakes, lizards, beautiful women, and wackily plumed birds; a floor below the terrarium, in burnt umber rooms, the noble Virgil Thompson, composer, deaf as the snakes above him, surrounded by picture-crowded walls; Arthur Miller, typing away on his play in progress, *After the Fall*; another Arthur, Clarke, writing the novel *2001*; another Clarke, Shirley, filming her documentary, *Portrait of Jason*; Andy Warhol shooting *Chelsea Girls*; Peter Brook preparing *Marat/Sade*; Ken Tynan reviewing for the New Yorker and reviewing nightly his marriage to Elaine Dundy; Viva, superstar; super painters de Kooning, Alechinsky, Dine, and Arman still in his black leather jacket; pushers and users of

heroin, cocaine, opium, Quaaludes, speed, mescaline, angel dust, LSD—okay, enough, I'm nauseous!—and transient hookers, male and female, indistinguishable from most of the permanent residents, plying a lively trade. It all gave me the feeling that this was an ideal place to raise a family . . . (p. 406-7)

He might well have mentioned two more Chelsea Hotel luminaries: Stanley Kubrick, who of course directed the movie version of Clarke's *2001: A Space Odyssey*, and Terry Southern, who wrote the screenplay for *Dr. Strangelove* (also directed by Kubrick), and who gave the title to Larry's most controversial work of art, "Lampman Loves It", a free-standing wood and Plexiglas sculpture depicting a Black man fucking a white Playboy Playmate (and later, partly on Frank O'Hara's advice, a generic white man) from behind with a long, Christmas bulb-tipped penis.

Despite his disdain for skylights, you gotta believe that Rivers, who died in 2002, would've agreed that the Chelsea Hotel is too culturally significant to be turned into just another generic party warehouse—rooms from $500-$6000, with five bars planned for the ground floor alone—which is the direction we seem to be going in lately. Though his apartment was on the third floor, when he later obtained a studio on the ninth floor, down the hall from Virgil Thompson, the first painting he executed in the Chelsea, "Moon Man and Moon Lady", featuring Village Voice dance critic (and *Lesbian Nation* author) Jill Johnston as the lady, boasts both the appropriate grandeur and the requisite other-worldly flavor that the Bard Family's renowned "Rest Stop for Rare Individuals" demands.

DAVID COLLARD

A Good Innings

I n *The Hatred of Poetry* (Fitzcarraldo Editions, 2016) Ben Lerner wrote that 'poetry isn't hard. It's impossible' and this, he argued, is because the 'abstract potential' of a poem is compromised when it becomes part of the world, that the creation of poetry is in itself a betrayal of the original impulse to write. So, he continues, all poets are destined to fail and to fail as a poet is to fail not only artistically but also existentially.

It's fair to say that although he was not by any means a failure Kenneth Allott (1912–1973) did not fulfil his early promise as a poet and is today best known, if at all, for the much-anthologised 'Lament for a Cricket Eleven', first published when he was 26. One of the finest poems of the Thirties, this is an existential score card recording the various fates of a group of young cricketers photographed in 1905.

LAMENT FOR A CRICKET ELEVEN*

Beyond the edge of the sepia
Rises the weak photographer
With the moist moustaches and the made-up tie.
He looked with his mechanical eye,
And the upshot was that they had to die.

Portrait of the Eleven nineteen-o-five
To show when these missing persons were last alive.
Two sit in Threadneedle Street like gnomes.
One is a careless schoolmaster
Busy with carved desks, honour and lines.
He is eaten by a wicked cancer.
They have detectives to watch their homes.

From the camera hood he looks at the faces
Like the spectral pose of the praying mantis.
Watch for the dicky-bird. But, oh my dear,
That bird will not migrate this year.
Oh for a parasol, oh for a fan
To hide my weak chin from the little man.

One climbs mountains in a storm of fear,
Begs to be unroped and left alone.
One went mad by a tape-machine.
One laughed for a fortnight and went to sea.
Like a sun one follows the jeunesse dorée.

With his hand on the bulb he looks at them.
The smiles on their faces are upside down.
'I'll turn my head and spoil the plate.'
'Thank you, gentlemen.' Too late. Too late.

* (c) the Estate of Kenneth Allott and Salt Publishing, with permission.

One greyhead was beaten in a prison riot.
He needs injections to keep him quiet.
Another was a handsome clergyman,
But mortification has long set in.
One keeps six dogs in an unlit cellar.
The last is a randy bachelor.

The photographer in the norfolk jacket
Sits upstairs in his darkroom attic.
His hand is expert at scissors and pin.
The shadows lengthen, the days draw in,
And the mice come out round the iron stove.
'What I am doing, I am doing for love.
When shall I burn this negative
And hang the receiver up on grief?'

The Great War is never explicitly mentioned, although that 'storm of fear' is certainly suggestive. The troubled ex-cricketers (and future ex-servicemen) will all become social outcasts, misfits prone to ennui, illness, criminality and insanity, while the photographer himself becomes an avatar of the Grim Reaper: 'He looked with his mechanical eye, And the upshot was that they had to die.'

The poem came to mind recently when I acquired a copy of *New Oxford Poetry 1936*, one of fifty deluxe editions published by Basil Blackwell. A slim octavo in decorated boards, it features one of Allott's earliest appearances in print. My copy (number 20) has been signed by all twenty-seven contributors—one pictures a crowded room more than eighty years ago, filled with chattering laughter as each young poet waits in line to sign the book that bears his or her name. There's a light haze of cigarette smoke, the clink of glasses.

'Oxford Poetry is dead' is the disarming claim of the editor Alastair Sandford in his introduction, but it turns out he is referring to the title of the original series of annual collections first published in 1910. *Oxford Poetry* had an illustrious succession of editors and an even more illustrious roster of contributors, but the publication had been subject to a four-year hiatus prior to this relaunch which is, the editor continues, 'a resurrection, perhaps even a renascence'. The break in publication coincided with the emergence of a new generation of poets and Sandford confirms that submissions to this volume reflected two opposing schools: 'there were sufficient "perfumes of yestereen" and "darkling cloisters" in the rejected MSS, to say nothing of "armpit fogs" and "public-lavatory smells," to make one believe it is a fairly representative selection.' It certainly is, and offers a fascinating snapshot of poetic and cultural allegiances in Oxford between the wars.

Fifteen of the contributors were out-and-out modernists, five more submitted verses in the approved Georgian manner with 'darkling cloisters' a-plenty while the rest wavered between the two, their modernist sensibilities and subject matter expressed within long-established prosodic forms. Fifteen years after the appearance of 'The Love Song of J. Alfred Prufrock', Eliot was still an overwhelming influence on the first group and J.E. Banbury (Magdalen College) falls somewhere between homage and plagiarism in his 'Record':

The lilt of some suburban gramophone
Trickles along the street
Measuring with half-heard rhythm and tone
The unrelated tread of daily feet.

Other young modernists offer similar Eliotian passages about, well, passages, and wet streets, fog, urban dinginess, neurological malaise and moral squalor are all deployed and explored with relish. In stark contrast those poets loyal to the Georgian movement turn out well-crafted lyrics about nature, abstract love, virtue and loyalty.

Technically competent, decidedly dull, these reflect the way poetry was taught by schoolmasters born in the previous century who had grown up on a diet of Tennyson, Browning and other eminent Victorians. Let David Graham (another Magdalen man) stand for them all with 'Men as Trees Walking':

Silent and stiff and green,
  The trees against the sky
Seemed but a painted screen
  And still the men went by,

March-marching away
  The men were marching still
And still it seemed but a play
  That surely would end. Until

A tired evening breeze
  Woke in the summer sky
Spoke to the canvas trees
  And moved them to a sigh.

This kind of poetry would find no place in *The Faber Book of Modern Verse*, also published in 1936. The editor Michael Roberts conceded in his introduction that many of the 'difficult or irritating' poems he included would prompt feelings of animosity in some readers; Auden and Eliot were praised but Robert Frost and Thomas Hardy omitted.

Allott opens *New Oxford Poetry 1936* with 'The Albatross', an exercise in surrealist whimsy which appears never to have been republished and concludes thus:

> Waiter a kind word and a double whiskey
> waiter an ostrich feather for the lady
> but now I remember the waiters have all gone home
> and now the Duchess' hair is coming down.

He would next appear in *The Year's Poetry 1937* alongside the four MacSpaundays and other major poets British and European, living and dead. His stylish debut collection *Poems* was published by the Hogarth Press the following year and includes 'Exodus', which features these very Audenesque lines:

> From this wet island of birds and chimneys
> Who can watch suffering Europe and not be angry?
> For death can hardly be ridiculous,
> And the busking hysteria of our rulers,
> Which seemed so funny to our fathers,
> Dirties the newsreels for us.

He was by now, according to Richard Hoggart (employing a cricketing term) a member of the 'First Eleven' of poets surrounding Auden, but also among the handful of 1930s poets who were able to absorb Auden's influence without becoming mere imitators.

From Autumn 1941 he was co-editor of *Kingdom Come: the magazine of war-time Oxford* which, partly financed by the family planning campaigner Marie Stopes, was known to wags as 'Condom King'. During the War Allott was increasingly recognised as a rising young poet—Francis Scarfe dedicated a chapter to him in *Auden and After* (1942), one of the first books to engage critically with the Auden generation of poets. A second collection, *The Ventriloquist's Doll*, was published by Cresset Press in 1943 but that, poetically speaking, was that. Allott all but abandoned

poetry and during the next three decades wrote just sixteen poems and published even fewer.

Was this a principled renunciation, or something less considered, less momentous? Was it a commitment to failure? After the war Allott worked as a teacher and, from 1948 until his death from lung cancer in 1973, as a lecturer in English literature at the University of Liverpool. He became an authority on Matthew Arnold, wrote a biography of Jules Verne, adapted E.M. Forster's novel *A Room with a View* for the stage and edited *The Penguin Book of Contemporary Verse* (1950), which became a college staple. His *Collected Poems* appeared posthumously in 1975, and a revised edition, published by Salt in 2008, gathered a further 34 uncollected poems.

It was a distinguished literary career, but his current poetic status is uncertain. The reasons behind Allott's almost complete break with poetry prompt our speculation. Was he, as the poet Bernard Gutteridge claimed in the 1940s, 'too modish, too bright . . . cynical and over clever' to attract a general audience after the war? Did he succumb to a sense of personal poetic irrelevance and redundancy? There were personal travails (divorce, a loss of faith) and it seems likely that, faced with momentous social, political and personal upheavals, Allott found it difficult—or impossible—to move away from his established surrealist style to something plainer, more direct and socially engagé. He seems to anticipate the dilemma in the opening of 'Steering Line' from his second collection:

> The war mismanages time,
> Out of the windows goes love.
> We shall never be even now.
> All emotions are blurred,
> Gas-jets seen through a fog,
> Ecstasy tapped like a tree,
> Ecstasy dripping away
> And life swims out of the slide.

Donald Davie, lecturing in 1980, argued persuasively for Allott's continuing poetic commitment after 1943 but his case was based on, and therefore weakened by, that meagre output. In the uncollected poem 'Barking' (c. 1933) Allott pre-empts any such claim and is ironically self-effacing about his poetic range and cultural presence:

> I have a few hundred words and a half-dozen themes
> and pleasure of them whether you will or no.
> Among coughing howitzers and grunting tractors
> I tinkle a modest teaspoon in a cup.

Other poetical careers were disrupted by the War—Gavin Ewart graduated from Cambridge in 1936 and published his first collection *Poems and Songs* in 1939 after which nothing followed until *Londoners* in 1964; Laura Riding gave up writing poetry soon after the publication of her *Collected Poems* in 1938 but felt unable to explain her reasons for several decades, eventually claiming that there was an 'absolute incompatibility' between what she terms the 'craft' and the 'creed' of poetry. According to Tom Fisher 'her departure from poetry was precipitated by a reading of modernism as both the fulfilment and undoing of what she considered poetry's promise and possibility.' This, one might think, was and is a feeling shared by many writers, a version of Harold Bloom's 'Anxiety of Influence'. But is renunciation a strategy or an abdication?

The only other *New Oxford* contributor with a substantial literary career was the American **Paul Engle** (1908–1991) a Rhodes Scholar at Merton College. His 'POEM I' and 'POEM II' were lucid exercises in rhymed dimeter, the former of which opens:

> Let no longer
> In time's curved run
> The living linger
> When is only
> Glitter of gun
> And cruel life lonely
> For the rib sheath.

In 1941 Engle became director of the Iowa Writers' Workshop (a position he held for twenty-five years) and founder of the International Writing Programme, both at the University of Iowa. These became the model for hundreds of later writing programmes around the world. Engle would influence generations of writers from Flannery O'Connor to Raymond Carver, and have parallel careers as a poet, editor, teacher, literary critic, novelist, and playwright. He never became a cele-

brated poet because (according to Lewis Turco's entry in the *Oxford Companion to Modern Poetry*) 'he attempted generally to be popular rather than literary'. Kurt Vonnegut described him in a letter to friends as 'a hayseed clown, a foxy grandpa, a terrific promoter, who, if you listen closely, talks like a man with a paper asshole'.

Allott and Engle both have their place in literary history, but what of the other contributors to *Oxford Poetry 1936*? I assumed that some would continue to write and perhaps even to publish poetry, so I chose nine of them at random, adding them to Allott and Engle to form a cricketing eleven. Then I began to dig.

The anthology's editor **Alastair Wallace Sandford** (1916–1971), the son of a wealthy Australian businessman and politician, became a barrister in Adelaide after graduating from Balliol and enlisted in the Australian army in 1941, working as a member of the intelligence corps in the Middle East. The war came as a disruption though not, for him, a catastrophic one. He rose to the rank of colonel and after the war worked for British Petroleum, spending the rest of his life in Italy. He was appointed CBE in 1968, and appears to have made no further mark on poetry.

His co-editor **Alan Rook** (1909–1990) was a member of St. Catherine's Society, a non-residential college with buildings in St Aldate's, precursor to St. Catherine's College, founded in 1962. Rook served with the Royal Artillery, was stationed in Egypt during the war and became part of a loose-knit community of Cairo poets. Along with John Gawsworth and John Waller he formed the 'Salamander' group and was a prolific wartime poet, publishing three collections: *Soldiers, This Solitude* (1942), *These Are My Comrades* (1943) and *We Who Are Fortunate* (1945). In peace time he became a wine merchant and in 1964 planted the world's most northerly vineyard at Stragglethorpe Hall in Lincolnshire, producing 2,000 bottles of dry white Lincoln Imperial annually.

Sydney Carter (1915–2004) later became a songwriter and part of the post-war folk music revival. A conscientious pacifist, he had served with the Friends' Ambulance Unit in Egypt, Palestine and Greece alongside Donald Swann (of Flanders & Swann fame) with whom he collaborated. As a performer he appeared alongside Martin Carthy, Ewan MacColl, Pete Seeger and Judy Collins. As a prolific songwriter he is best known for providing words to the Shaker tune 'Simple Gifts' ('Dance, then,wherever you may be / I am the Lord of the Dance, said he'), a song so deeply embedded in our culture that it is surprising to learn it was written only fifty years ago. He was also involved in the satire boom of the 1960s, contributing to the BBC's *That Was the Week That Was*. His 'Friday Morning' included the lines 'It's God they ought to crucify / Instead of you and me . . .' which prompted Enoch Powell to call for it to be banned. 'My Last Cigarette', an ode to lung cancer performed by Sheila Hancock, featured on a 1962 album and was a minor hit. Carter's only poetry collection *Love More or Less* (1971) was described by Michael Grosvenor Myer in *English Dance and Song* as the work of 'an impressive spokesman for the believer in an age of general unbelief'.

After graduating from Keble **Peter Dwyer** (1911–1972) worked for 20th Century Fox films and Movietone News until 1939, when he was recruited by MI6 and began a career that could have been plotted by Graham Greene. He was based in Paris until the fall of France when he was transferred first to Panama and then to the Washington embassy, as South American expert for British Security Co-ordination (BSC). In this capacity he preceded the Cambridge double agent Kim Philby who took over the role of station chief in September 1949. It was Dwyer who identified the atomic spy Klaus Fuchs in what Philby (in *My Silent War*, 1968) called 'a brilliant piece of analysis'. On retiring as a spy, Dwyer crossed the Atlantic to join Canada's National Research Council and, in 1969, was appointed director of the Arts section of the Canada Council, the government funding body for the arts and humanities, a post he held for two years. His name lives on in the Pe-

ter Dwyer scholarship for the most promising student at the National Ballet School in Ottawa, but it is a minor mystery why someone who received the Order of Canada (two months before he died) does not appear to have attracted any official obituary.

Henry Gifford (1913–2003) studied Classics at Christ Church and from 1936 worked for two years in a camp for Spanish Civil War refugees in North London. He taught for a term at Eton and in 1940 was commissioned in the Royal Armoured Corps, serving in the Middle East and Germany. He learned Russian while on active service and after the war became a distinguished scholar as Professor of English and Comparative Literature at Bristol, pioneering Russian Studies as a discipline in British universities.

In a very long life—he died age 99 in 2006—**Patrick Howarth** (St. John's) was variously a soldier, journalist, diplomat, biographer, historian, and traveller. His colourful career also involved banana-growing in Fiji and parachute expeditions to the North Pole. Piers Plowright's engaging *Independent* obituary includes the following, about Howarth's time in Poland in the late 1930s:

> He also managed to play tennis for Britain, since the British Davis Cup team was prevented from attending the Polish national championships by the possibility of war. When it came, Howarth got out by the skin of his teeth and joined the Army in time to defend Bognor beach from invasion, moving on to Gibraltar and his only stab at pantomime. Howarth wrote 17 biographies and travel books before returning to poetry in the 1960s with Playback of a Lifetime, a verse memoir broadcast on BBC Radio 3 in 1974 after which a flood of poems followed, often at the rate of one a day. Diagnosed with terminal cancer he surprised and delighted his friends by living for a further three years.

'It was,' said Plowright, 'as if the poems were keeping him alive and a broadcast on Radio 3 of some of them [. . .] brought him immense pride and peace of mind'.

Rufus Noel-Buxton (1917–1980) served as an officer in the Artists Rifles and was invalided out of the army in 1940. He later worked in Oxford at the Agricultural Economics Institute, lectured with HM Forces, became a BBC producer and in

1948 succeeded to the title of 2nd Baron Noel-Buxton, of Aylsham in Norfolk. There followed a stint on the staff of *Farmer's Weekly*, after which he wrote a book (*Westminster Wader, being an Estimate of Westminster in All Ages, by one who longs for Muddy Water, and the return of the bittern to London Fen*, 1957) and later, as a Labour peer, seems to have risen without trace.

Margaret Stanley-Wrench (1916–1974) was one of only two women in the anthology (the other was her fellow Somerville College undergraduate **Margaret E. Rhodes**). She won the Newdigate Prize in 1937 for 'The Man in the Moon' which was widely re-printed and anthologised although, according to Jane Dowson in *Women's Poetry of the 1930s: A Critical Anthology*, the poem 'may raise questions about the criteria for prizewinning, but it was nevertheless an achievement.' She befriended the poet Keith Douglas in the 1930s and in 1938 published a first collection *News Reel and Other Poems* (Macmillan), described by one reviewer as 'vivid and arresting'. She wrote biographies of Thomas More, Edward the Confessor and Chaucer, a play for mannequins and, in the early 1950s, published two popular books for children: *The Rival Riding Schools* and *How Much for a Pony?*. A second poetry collection *A Tale for the Fall of the Year* appeared in 1959 and a modern English version of Chaucer's *Troilus and Criseyde* in 1965.

John Short (1911–1991) was born in the Lake District town of Ambleside to working-class parents. A bright child, he was awarded a scholarship to Keswick Grammar School but left early owing to financial difficulties, finding employment as a grocer, commercial traveller and landscape gardener and eventually working with the Church Army until his health broke down. He later obtained an Extra-mural Scholarship to Balliol College. He contributed two poems to *New Oxford Poetry*, the first and better of which the incantatory 'Six Ladder-steps for Lent':

From a furnace rake out ash
In those clinkers set thy feet

For whips of scorn thy breast to slash
Tear up a pauper's winding-sheet

Next beside a pin-shaft tread
Rise by crawling down a seam

Spin thy hopes from common thread
And stretch prayer's weft upon that beam

Macerations feed the soul
Vow a means-test rule and see

Seven Easter jonquils snow-bright and tall
Dance in passion's cemetery.

Short would appear with Allott in *The Year's Poetry 1937* and his poems were broadcast by the BBC and published in *The Listener* and *English Poems of Tomorrow*. After the war (in which he fought, though details are scant) he returned to his home town where he settled in a wooden workmen's cottage near Lake Windermere. According to a local resident 'he lived a simple life. He was poorly dressed, jobless, often drunk, but with a cultured voice which commanded respect from local people.' He would sometimes earn a few pounds by washing dishes at a local hotel. The poet Vernon Scannell (1922–2007) admired Short's only collection *The Oak and the Ash* (published by Dent in 1947) and made a point of seeking him out during a visit to Ambleside in 1978. It was, according to the younger poet (as reported in James Andrew Taylor's Scannell biography *Walking Wounded*), an awkward encounter:

> I could just see the pale blur of the old face, the watchful, timid eyes peering from the shadows. For what seemed a long time he didn't speak and I was beginning to think our visit was futile when he muttered something I couldn't catch and then opened the door just wide enough for him to slip through and close it behind him. Clearly he didn't want me to see inside his hovel.

All Short wanted to talk about, and obsessively, was a complicated legal affair in which he claimed to have been cheated out of a substantial inheritance. He flatly refused to discuss his poetry and Scannell left, disappointed by this 'trampish little hermit' but with his admiration for the work undimmed. Short's fate is too close to Allott's doomed cricketers for comfort.

Scannell has an entry in the *Oxford Companion to Modern Poetry*, as do Allott and Engle. Short and Rook and Stanley-Wrench do not. Who can say what prompted their desire to write poetry, and the decision—if it was a decision—to stop? Some gave up poetry, others were given up by it, although the idea of a capricious muse withholding her inspiration seems rather old hat. If by failure we mean a lack of public acclaim then most writers are, or in time become, failures.

We all of us achieve failure sooner or later, in one way or another, our innings ending with a long walk back to the pavilion as the shadows lengthen. Let us optimistically suppose that all of the contributors to *New Oxford Poetry 1936*, among the brightest and best of their generation, led fulfilling lives and made their mark without being poets, or writing poetry, and that some continued to find in poetry a source of purpose, satisfaction and consolation. To fail as a poet is not, *pace* Lerner, to fail as a human being. More than that, it's not even to fail as a poet because if, as Lerner sees it, all poetry is a failure then failure is a necessary *prerequisite* of poetry. That there are degrees of failure, that it's possible to fail better, is what keeps us reading, and poets writing. It is, one might even say, what poetry is for.

THomas WaLton

Unsavory Thoughts

For God's sakes

My friend enjoys things without writing about them. I find this fascinating. Not that I live my life to write about it—I don't—but it's baffling to me how my friend is able to just let events go. For him they simply disappear. Poof. He remembers them, but that's it. No diary or journal entry, no poem or essay. Nothing. Just a few memories that rarely rise to the surface.

I'm not suggesting my way is better. By all accounts, my friend seems happy enough. Happier than I am in fact. His by-all-appearances-positive attitude is enviable.

He's married. In his sixties. Has two grown kids. He's retired now and financially secure. He and his wife travel: Japan, the Dordogne, Mexico, Ireland. He loves his cat. Goes fishing. Crabbing. Rides his bike to the pub . . . He writes about none of it.

Perhaps he's enlightened. Or perhaps he just doesn't enjoy writing. Maybe I'm too attached to this world. Maybe I'm trying too hard to slow it down as it slips quickly out from under me. I admire his lack of anxiety. His lack of urgency. He doesn't write a single thing! He does crossword puzzles for god's sakes! And he does them calmly, as if it isn't a supreme waste of time.

I'm afraid that when I'm in my sixties all I'll be doing is writing. Frantically writing. Sitting in a chair somewhere, desperately taking notes on what I see out the window, cataloguing as many memories as possible: the dogwood leaves turning orange, a rain just beginning, the neighbor who moved into the apartment across the street after Kevin left, the circumstances of Kevin's leaving, someone else named Kevin taking his place. I'll end up like Henry Darger, alone in a room somewhere, madly documenting the instances where the weatherman got the weather wrong, even if only by a degree or two.

What weird narcissism is this? That stares out and records data on the brick buildings, the gray sky, the workers removing the telephone pole where the little girl named Naima used to live:

"Like the Coltrane song," I said when I met them, but the parents didn't know the reference. "She's not named after the song?"

"No, we just liked the name . . ."

"Do you still like it?"

"Yes, of course. What do you mean?"

"I'm not sure. You said you liked it . . . do you still?"

"Still what?"

"Like the name, Naima?"

"Of course we like the name, she's our daughter!"

That was several months ago. They haven't spoken to me since, other than to smile and turn away, which I suppose says a lot.

Wrought iron rails wrap around my friend's front balcony, geraniums spill down in brilliant platitudes. By fall they're wasted, neglected for weeks, mostly dead, brown and leggy, hanging over the gutters in the cold evening air. None of this bothers him.

I love my friend. I confess, I'm weirdly jealous. He is living a literal life, simple and direct, whereas I can't escape the metaphors. I see myself in everything, in everything some part of me (usually my mortality). Every instance is both that instance and the symbolic representation of other instances.

We go to a gallery, my life hangs on every wall, and it *is* every wall, and it is also the gallery itself. My friend sees none of it. He has a great time. He smiles, laughs, suggests we go for a beer.

At the pub we talk about the paintings . . . I could talk about them for hours, but he says only, "I liked them. They were nice." He is more interested in the beer, the mirror hanging over the bar, and the young couple arguing at a small table in the corner. All of which he'll forget, and I will write down in a notebook tomorrow. For whom? For what? I've no idea.

On Happiness; Query for a Non-fiction Book

"... all are of the dust, and all turn to dust again."
—Ecclesiastes 3:20

Dear Esteemed Literary Agent,

I'm writing a book on happiness. It will be a very short book. Or a very long book (I have the ordinary talent of being able to go on forever), and full of lies. The first line will be "This book is full of lies." Or perhaps that will be the title: On Happiness; A Book of Lies. Subtitles very much remain in these days. They are perpetually trending. I think because no one has the confidence to simply title their book. We're too self-conscious, too unwilling to stick our necks out. Which reminds me, why do all the headshots of literary agents look as if they're real estate agents? All of you look like a bunch of clay busts who wouldn't know the first thing about great literature, or even good literature, mere literature. What the hell are you trying to "represent" anyway? Maybe you should just sell houses . . . but I digress.

My book *On Happiness; A Book of Lies* will be short, or long, and full of lies. The sun will, however, figure greatly, but not too much of it. And nature in its most bucolic and pastoral guise. The way Raphael imagined it. Nature of the Renaissance. None of this Ikkyu baloney ("nature's a killer I won't sing to it"). None of these hurricanes and droughts, floods, etc. Those are not elements of happiness but of emptiness. And no moon. The moon doesn't belong in a book on happiness. Even one full of lies.

It will be a funny book, but not sarcastic. Everyone will die. A wholesome comedic thread will run through the book. Something like the anodyne comedians of the 1950s, or Jim Gaffigan. Dumb jokes will abound. But funny jokes. Nothing like Jim Gaffigan (unless you think he's funny). I will punctuate each chapter with a joke that summarizes in a pithy way the concepts laid out in that chapter. Something like (at the end of the chapter on alcoholic parents for instance) "my father drank so much scotch when I was a kid that I thought hopscotch was a cruel imitation of my drunk dad stumbling home from the bar."

Perhaps that's too dark. The jokes in my happiness book will be much lighter. There will be a butterfly in every punch line. And hummingbirds and flowers. "What did the butterfly say to the hummingbird? I'm not a flower, please take that thing out of my asphodel!"

In my book *On Happiness*, the jokes will be better than that.

In my book *On Happiness*, all the Harley Davidsons will be electric. All the literary agents will look like Paul Verlaine just before he shot Rimbaud. It will only rain when you're in the mood for it, and when you have a window to look through. And you can be as fat as you want in your forties and no one will notice or care. There will be no exercise in my book. Or stretching. There will be no need for "self-care." In fact, carelessness will abound! More of this Ikkyu baloney ("sin like a madman until you can't do anything else").

In fact, that will be the gist of my book, its condensed milk, its deer dung squeezed diamond-like straight out the rump: the world's full of lies, no one cares, it will all be over soon, so be fucking happy.

Please let me know if you or your agency would be interested in representing such a project.

A Note on My Favorite Painting in One of the (Increasingly) Shitty Museums in My Town

A portrait of Bianca Maria Sforza hangs in the atrium at one of the local art museums. Most people walk past it without stopping to look.

It's unexceptional, or rather, exceptional only for the sad, sour look on the sitter's face. The painting is merely "art," as in, "we need to get some art for this atrium." It could be anything. And it is.

Because of this, it's one of my favorite paintings in the entire museum.

The museum is within walking distance from my apartment. I stop there whenever something new is showing, a few times a year. It's a small museum, and unfortunately one that's become increasingly, debilitatingly self-conscious. One that suffers from acute evaluation anxiety. Why have so many museums become so enormously worried about how they will appear to the public? Are our politics right? Are we offending anyone? Rather than a curator with a clear vision of what they want to show their patrons, these curators have no vision, and try instead to guess at what the public might want to see. To guess at what the portion of the public that doesn't even like art wants to see. It's a kind of feckless display of flaccid vision, and results in a weird pablum of safe messaging and mediocrity: art that seems to be valued only on whether it conforms to whatever is currently the bumper sticker slogan du jour.

The portrait of Bianca Maria Sforza is, by contrast, an afterthought. It is thoughtless, nearly unintentional. It's mere decoration. Less an *objet d'art* than an object to fill a space. They just needed something on the wall. It could've been a plant, or a coat rack. I love it!

I've come to appreciate this type of accidental, thoughtless display. It's far better than what passes these days as thoughtful intention, certainly when that thoughtful intention is meant only to cater to a public that has no sense of art, no faith in art, in fact despises art, and thinks art should have the role only of reinforcing certain cliché sociopolitical and moral values and very little (if anything) else.

A Letter from the Coast

Seeking to smell utterly delightful, of far-flung
oils and extravagant perfumes that together constitute the fact of my
	cachet,
I arrived upon this unknown shore.

A keen wind blew, as if released from a miniature giant's coin purse;
there lay, partly submerged in the sand, seashells as large as motorcycle
	sidecars;
and I knew not my location amid the lagoons.

Damn that coachman, who deposited me so unceremoniously at the
	riverhead!

The sun above was dressed in tatters and the crabs all scuttled to their
parlor rooms.
From my rucksack, I withdrew my pistol: a gift of my late employer's
	daughter.
"Oh, my darling Martha, if only I were with you now."
Yet, the pistol would not fire; its gearings, it seemed, were clotted with
	barnacles.

I am more than anything a man of letters.
I have with the power of will threaded licorice straws through the eye of a
	needle.
Still, I heard the death knell of my fate echo along the coastline.
I stumbled, lost to despair, mere kibble for the seabirds.

In my trouser pocket, I found a crumpled sheaf of paper.
I wrote my name upon it.
I wrote, "Thomas Jefferson, a nobody."

Contributors

P.J. Blumenthal, an American writer in Munich, Germany, writes in both German and English. He is the author of a non-fiction book on feral man, *Kaspar Hausers Geschwister* (Kaspar Hauser's Siblings), and a German-language blog, "Der Sprachbloggeur."

Israel A. Bonilla lives in Guadalajara, Jalisco. His work has appeared in *Able Muse*, *New World Writing*, *BULL*, *Hawk & Whippoorwill*, *Expanded Field*, *FEED*, *ONE ART*, *Letralia*, and elsewhere. His debut micro-chapbook, *Landscapes*, is part of Ghost City Press's 2021 Summer Series.

Jesi Buell is an artist from Upstate New York. Under the name Jesi Bender, she helms KERNPUNKT Press, a home for experimental writing. She is the author of Dangerous Women (dancing girl press, 2022), *KINDERKRANKENHAUS* (Sagging Meniscus, 2021) and *The Book of the Last Word* (Whiskey Tit 2019). Her shorter writing has appeared in *The Rumpus*, *Split Lip*, *Adroit Journal*, and elsewhere.

Marvin Cohen is the author of many novels, plays, and collections of essays, stories, and poems. He lives on the Lower East Side of Manhattan.

David Collard, writer, critic and researcher, is the author of *Multiple Joyce* (Sagging Meniscus, 2022). A regular contributor to the *Times Literary Supplement*, the *Literary Review* and many other publications, he organizes and hosts cultish online gatherings.

Chase Dayton lives in Texas with himself and others.

Debra Di Blasi is the author of ten books, including *Selling the Farm: Descants from a Recollected Past*, winner of the 2019 C&R Press Nonfiction Award. She is a former publisher, educator and art critic now dividing her time between the US and Portugal. "Little Pricks" is excerpted from her novel, *Birth of Eros*, forthcoming 2022 from KERNPUNKT Press.

Mark DuCharme is the author of *We, the Monstrous: Script for an Unrealizable Film*, *Counter Fluencies 1-20*, *The Unfinished: Books I-VI*, *Answer*, *The Sensory Cabinet* and other works. *Scorpion Letters* will be published as a chapbook by Ethel in 2022. His poetry has appeared widely in such venues as *BlazeVOX*, *Caliban Online*, *Colorado Review*, *Eratio*, *First Intensity*, *Indefinite Space*, *New American Writing*, *Noon*, *Otoliths*, *Shiny*, *Talisman*, *Unlikely Stories*, *Word/ for Word*, and *Poetics for the More-Than-Human World: An Anthology of Poetry and Commentary*. A recipient of the Neodata Endowment in Literature and the Gertrude Stein Award in Innovative American Poetry, he lives in Boulder, Colorado.

Benjamin McPherson Ficklin is the author of the chapbook *A Cynical View of Dystopian America.* Their work has been published in *Lomography, wildness, Ursus Americanus Press, Cheap Pop, STORGY, Clackamas Literary Review, Tahoma Literary Review, Autre, Autonomous Press, Oregon Voice Magazine*, and recognized in *Best Small Fiction 2019* and *Best American Essays 2020*.

Jack Foley's numerous books of poetry, fiction and criticism include *Visions and Affiliations*, a "chronoencyclopedia" of California poetry from 1940 to 2005, *Grief Songs* (SM, 2017) and *When Sleep Comes* (SM, 2020). He lives in Oakland and hosts a weekly radio show, *Cover to Cover*, on Berkeley's Pacifica station, KPFA.

Ed Hamilton was born in Atlanta, Georgia, and grew up in Louisville, Kentucky. Ed is the author of three books: a non-fiction work, *Legends of the Chelsea Hotel: Living with the Artists and Outlaws of New York's Rebel Mecca* (Da Capo/Perseus, 2007); a short story collection, *The Chintz Age: Tales of Love and Loss for a New New York* (Červená Barva Press), which spent 10 months on the Small Press Best Sellers List in 2016; and a novel, *Lords of the Schoolyard* (Sagging Meniscus, 2018), which was nominated for a Pushcart Prize. His short fiction has appeared in dozens of small journals, including: *Limestone Journal, The Journal of Kentucky Studies, SoMa Review, River Walk Journal, Exquisite Corpse, Bohemia, Modern Drunkard, Omphalos*, and in translation in the Czech Republic's *Host*. His non-fiction has appeared in *The Villager, Chelsea Now, The Huffington Post*, and *Living With Legends: Hotel Chelsea Blog*. Ed lives in New York City.

John Patrick Higgins is a playwright, short story writer, screenwriter and director. He lives in Belfast.

Tomoé Hill's work has appeared in such publications as *Socrates on the Beach*, *The London Magazine*, *Vol. 1 Brooklyn*, *3:AM Magazine*, *Music & Literature*, *Numéro Cinq*, and *Lapsus Lima*, as well as the anthologies *We'll Never Have Paris* (Repeater Books), *Azimuth* (Sonic Art Research Unit at Oxford Brookes University), and *Trauma: Essays on Art and Mental Health* (Dodo Ink). Her *Songs of Olympia*, essays in response to Michel Leiris' *The Ribbon at Olympia's Throat*, is forthcoming from Sagging Meniscus in 2023.

Paul Kavanagh wrote *Kitchen Sink* (Aiurea Press).

Kurt Luchs is the author of *Falling in the Direction of Up* (SM, 2020), *One of These Things Is Not Like the Other* (Finishing Line Press, 2019), and the humor collection *It's Funny Until Someone Loses an Eye (Then It's Really Funny)* (SM, 2017). He lives in Michigan.

Gabrielle McAree is a writer from Fishers, Indiana. Her work appears in *X-R-A-Y*, *Berkeley Fiction Review*, *Reflex Press*, *The Molotov Cocktail*, and elsewhere. She lives in NYC and is on Twitter @gmcaree_.

Alan McCormick lives in Wicklow, Ireland. His writing has been widely published, including in *Best British Short Stories*, *Popshot*, *Cōnfingō Magazine*, and *A Wild and Precious Life—A Recovery Anthology*; and online at *3:AM Magazine*, *The Quietus*, *Words for the Wild*, *Fictive Dream*, *Dead Drunk Dublin* and *Époque Press*.

R.S. Mengert completed an MFA in poetry at Syracuse University. His work has appeared in *Pensive*, *SurVision*, *Zymbol*, *Poor Yorick*, *Maintenant*, *Poetry is Dead*, *ABZ*, *Four Chambers*, *The Café Review*, *Fjords*, *San Pedro River Review*, and *Enizagam*. He lives in Tempe, AZ, with his wife and an unusually loud cat.

Tracie Morris is the author of several books and is a poet, professor, performer, voice teacher and theorist. She is a professor at the Iowa Writers' Workshop.

M.J. Nicholls is the author of the novels *Condemned to Cymru* (SM, 2022), *Trimming England* (SM, 2021), *Scotland Before the Bomb* (SM, 2019), The *1002nd Book to Read Before You Die* (SM, 2018), *The Quiddity of Delusion* (SM, 2017), *The House of Writers* (SM, 2016), and *A Postmodern Belch* (2014). He lives in Glasgow.

David Rose, born 1949, resident in Britain, is now retired after a working life in the Post Office. His short stories are published widely in the UK and US, including in *The Penguin Book of the Contemporary Short Story* (ed. Philip Hensher, 2018) and partly collected in *Posthumous Stories* (Salt, 2013). He is the author of two novels: *Vault* (Salt, 2011) and *Meridian* (Unthank Books, 2015).

Mike Silverton's poetry appeared in the late 60s and early 70s in *Harper's*, *The Nation*, *Wormwood Review*, *Poetry Now*, *some/thing*, *Chelsea*, *Prairie Schooner*, *Elephant* and elsewhere. William Cole included Mike's poems in four anthologies: *Eight Lines and Under* (Macmillan, 1967), *Pith and Vinegar* (Simon and Schuster, 1969), *Poetry Brief* (Macmillan, 1971), and *Poems One Line & Longer* (Grossman, 1973).

Will Stanier currently lives in Tucson where he is training to be a librarian. He is the author of a chapbook, *Everything Happens Next* (Blue Arrangements, 2021).His poems have appeared,or are forthcoming, in *Cleaver Magazine*, *Interim*, *Pacifica*, *Lazy Susan*, *The Volta*, and *RECLINER*.

Julian Stannard's most recent collection is *Heat Wave* (Salt, 2020).

Selin Tamtekin is a Turkish-British novelist and art writer based in London. She is a columnist for the Turkish news website, T24. Under the name Deniz Goran she has written two novels:*The Turkish Diplomat's Daughter*, published in 2007 in the UK and subsequently in translation in Turkey, Italy, Germany, Greece and Taiwan, and *The Fugitive of Gezi Park*, forthcoming in Spring 2023 in the UK from Ortac Press.

Thomas Walton is the author of four books: *Good Morning Bonecrusher!* (Spuyten Duyvil, 2021), *All the Useless Things Are Mine* (SM, 2020), *The World Is All That Does Befall Us* (Ravenna Press, 2019), and, with Elizabeth Cooperman, *The Last Mosaic* (SM, 2018). He lives in Seattle, where he edits *PageBoy Magazine*.

Dara Wier's forthcoming book is *Tolstoy Killed Anna Karenina* from Wave Books. She lives and works in Factory Hollow, MA.

www.ingramcontent.com/pod-product-compliance
Lightning Source LLC
Chambersburg PA
CBHW080820250626
47159CB00011B/3450